FERAL

.

FERAL

Returning to the Wild

Kyle Cooper Shrivastava

LIONANGEL
PRESS

This is a work of nonfiction. Nonetheless, some names and personal characteristics of the individuals involved have been changed in order to disguise their identities. Any resulting resemblance to persons living or dead is entirely coincidental and unintentional.

Paperback ISBN: 978-0-578-47393-2

Title-page art and cover photography by author
Editing: Izzy Martens, jokelife.com

ACKNOWLEDGMENTS

Thank you to Izzy Martens, Michelle Cooper, and Paul Shrivastava for your constant encouragement and meticulous editing. Thank you to my sister Claudia for being a writer I can look up to, and everyone who's read, discussed, partaken in, or inspired any of this material. My love goes out to all of you.

CONTENTS

FERAL

PREFACE

"Feral" isn't where this book began. Rather, it came together as an abstract collection of observations from years of studying and traveling. The word feral only arrived one day while I was looking through the dictionary in an attempt to translate the Wolof word "mala", which is used in Senegal to describe undomesticated animals. I had my own preconceptions about what "feral" meant, based on its typically negative connotation, however, reading its definition alone seemed to present a new meaning. In a way, it characterized in one word what was taking me several thousand.

"Feral" is defined as: **having escaped from domestication and become wild**. Try to take this at face value. Living in a modern American city, it's easy to feel as though we're almost overly domesticated. There's a social script within which we interact, and complex commercial systems that cater to every conceivable need or desire. It's a world that simultaneously serves us while feeding our dependence on it: this is the dynamic at the heart of domestication.

Yet despite our tacit acceptance of this dynamic, there exists for many the nagging suspicion that some natural psychological human needs aren't being met, a suspicion supported by rising rates of depression, anxiety, suicide, and drug addiction. Simultaneously, the immense complexity of our environment makes it incredibly difficult to critically examine our lives, to discern what's normal or even what's needed for us as humans (and perhaps more importantly animals).

So if there are aspects of our "domestic" lives that don't serve our mental well-being, how can we identify and address them? Can we determine the ways in which a "return to the wild" may benefit us, and if so, how can

1

we start down that path? This book will not provide concrete answers to these questions. Instead, it will attempt to add layers of nuance to the answers we already believe we have. This is an exercise in self-reflection, and while it may only generate additional questions, my hope is that it will also provide a rough guide, pointing in the direction of self-discovery and fulfillment.

There are, of course, multiple ways of looking at and understanding life, in which many seemingly contradictory truths exist. This book presents some of those truths and hopefully will allow people to discover others for themselves. I invite you to read with an open mind, seeking to discover how different perspectives fit together. I claim no authority over what's right, or what should be done. I only hope that, through self reflection, we are all enabled to create in our lives the changes we wish to someday see in the world.

PROLOGUE

What does it mean to be "wild"? We often first think of illogical, risky, or even criminal behavior, however these associations fail to holistically capture the essence and origin of the term. Wild animals by nature aren't illogical. As far as we know, they don't pointlessly stress, hate, desire, kill, or lament. They don't get caught up in the past or distracted by the future. They feel, they work, they strive, they build, and they do it all with a rationality directly focused on meeting their physical and psychological needs. They remain present in accomplishing their tasks, often with an almost meditative level of focus. They love, hate, and feel pleasure as well as pain, however, fail to excessively hold on to such feelings beyond their utility, as we often do. In this light, being wild means maintaining the passion that we value without the baggage that leads us into cycles of perpetual suffering.

The type of suffering that we term "existential suffering" is a trait that is unique to humans. Unlike universal external challenges such as hunger or violence, which are experienced throughout the animal kingdom, existential suffering is pain that we create for ourselves. It's a negative manifestation of our self-consciousness; a punishment we needlessly inflict upon our own minds. Fortunately, this also means we individually have the power to change. To become wild.

Human beings in all their complexity and understanding have strived for thousands of years through coordination, government, religion, spirituality, philosophy, and meditation to achieve a state of peace and happiness. Ironically, the closest we've come may have been the "wild" state in which we began.

Perhaps one of humanity's greatest faults has been believing our fundamental needs are different from the rest of the animal kingdom. We replace quality time with instant messages, substitute friendship with followers, forgo adventure for comfort, and sacrifice freedom for stuffy offices. While the wild, natural world is certainly full of challenges and harsh realities, it also embodies presence, genuine connection, adventure, and freedom. These qualities will always have more potential to bring us joy than the creature comforts and convenience we readily sacrifice them for.

PART ONE: WAITING

The Runner and The River Turtle

There was once a man who lived alone in a small wooden cabin deep in the forest. He dreamed of becoming the greatest distance runner in the world. The man would rise every morning, lace up his shoes, and jog for hours on end. He'd imagine his next race as he ran: the feeling of crossing the finish line, the sound of the crowd cheering, and the admiration of his friends.

He had run since he was a child, having always trailed behind his older brother, a successful track athlete. His brother had been the naturally strong, good-looking type, successful without having to put in much effort. For this, the man had always felt both admiration and resentment. On his runs, he would think back on the many times he came in second to his brother, the endless praise of their parents that was never directed at him, and even the little gifts he'd receive from family in consolation for being the perpetual runner-up.

One day as the man was running by the river, he saw a small turtle crawling along the bank. As he passed it, he thought to himself, "how horrible it must be to move so slowly," then continued on his way, the roar of future crowds echoing in his head. The next day the man once again came across the turtle, and again noticed its lack of speed and progress. He felt disdain towards the small animal as he sped by. When he passed the turtle for a third time that same evening, he felt inclined to stop.

Kneeling down, he whispered, "If you move like that you're never going to get anywhere."

The turtle looked back at him innocently. Then, to his surprise, it slowly replied, "I arrive with each step I take along this bank. You run for days and never reach your destination."

The man jumped back. "That's nonsense," he thought to himself. "I know just where I'm going and exactly how long it will take to get there."

The turtle shrugged its tiny head in and out of its shell.

"You're running in the past, towards the future. Those are the only two places to which you'll never arrive."

The man fell silent. Slowly, he rose, turned, and took one step away from the bank, then another, and another until he was deep in the forest. He walked all the way home that day, for the first time feeling the sun on the back of his neck and hearing the wind as it whistled gently through the tall pines.

Mindful-less

In recent years, the term mindfulness has become ubiquitous in the west. Despite this, our culture has made pragmatically understanding mindfulness and incorporating it into our everyday lives more difficult than ever. The intermittent buzzing of a phone in our pocket jolts us out of the present; the five thousand advertisements we're exposed to each day pull us into mental states of distracted craving.

This doesn't make mindfulness impossible, but it does complexify our path towards it. Since the modern barriers to mindfulness are phenomena that didn't exist in previous eras, we need to rethink what an impactful mindfulness practice looks like in the modern world and in our own individual lives.

To do this, we can approach mindfulness from a more accessible and relatable angle. Viewing it through a habit that we engage in on a daily basis – waiting. While mindfulness may feel abstract and difficult to grasp, waiting is common, simple, and identifiable. Its inherent place in the human experience makes our understanding of waiting an entry-point that can open a path forward for those struggling to feel the effects of meditation or understand esoteric spiritual texts.

To introduce the relationship between waiting and mindfulness, I'd like to tell the story of how I began connecting the two. A story I've titled: *realizing I had one foot in the grave before having ever really lived.*

Now with a name like that, you may be thinking I'm a banker or insurance salesman who's been grinding away behind a desk for the past 30 years, and that my solution is going to include some ecstasy, a tattoo, and a few weeks on a beach in Thailand. That may have made a great story, but it isn't mine. What made me realize I had one foot in the grave wasn't a lack of excitement, but rather an increased awareness of passing time.

I was sweating away an afternoon in my shadowy, electricity-less living room in the Liberian road town of Salala, listening to the yells of school children playing outside the elementary school across from my house, and thinking about an upcoming trip to Japan. I was exhausted, having just finished a particularly heavy workout to counteract the creeping stress of isolation common to international development workers. I hadn't had a hot shower or running water for six months and had eaten every combination of oil, rice, and hot pepper one could imagine. I wasn't unhappy. I loved my Liberian friends and neighbors. But it all felt tiring. In that moment, Japan seemed like an oasis, the relief needed for physical and mental rejuvenation. It was all I could think of, as I sat…and waited.

Then a thought occurred to me. There were seventeen days until I boarded my flight to Tokyo. While those seventeen days felt like a lifetime, I knew that when they were over, I would look back and all that time spent concentrating on the future would exist only as an unpleasant memory. The potential enjoyment of those seventeen days would be sacrificed and the memory of waiting retained. I then thought further into the future. I knew that after arriving in Japan, something inside me would dread returning to Liberia (not out of dislike for the country, but rather in the sense that we often wish our vacations could be extended). I worried this dread would cause me to focus on the number of days I had left in Japan before returning, reducing my enjoyment of my time there, and potentially even souring those memories. *Waiting in dread of returning* appeared to be equally damaging as *waiting in anticipation to leave*.

It was focusing on the future during both these "waiting periods" that would cause unhappiness. Focusing on leaving would prevent me from enjoying the days prior to my departure, and focusing on returning would reduce my enjoyment of the trip itself. A lack of presence would detract from each experience regardless of whether it was objectively difficult (waiting to leave) or pleasant (spending time on vacation).

If I continued on this path after returning, there would be more waiting for the next big event. Then the experience of that event would similarly be worsened by a focus on the fact that it would eventually end, a cycle that could go on forever. I thought, "If I wait for this trip right now, I'm going to spend my whole life waiting, and die having never done anything else." It was sickening, bringing on a bout of intense anxiety and fear. Was I on a path to perpetual waiting that could continue throughout my entire life?

In that moment, the present felt like a flame, slowly

burning its way across a long wick in a pitch-black room. The dancing light was the only thing visible and real. By focusing on the dark ahead or the ash left in its path, I would risk missing the beauty of the fire. This is the root of mindfulness.

I had been somewhat familiar with the idea of mindfulness before that moment. I had an intermittent mindfulness meditation practice, and had even led a mindfulness session at a psychological support retreat several years earlier. However, it was then that I made the transition from knowing to understanding.

From then on, mindfulness meant not waiting.

Waiting was living outside of the present. It was rejecting the reality of time, and allowing the mind to become preoccupied with memory or fantasy. Conversely, mindfulness was the mechanism through which perpetual waiting could be stopped and presence could be cultivated.

We often ponder what we need *to do* to be mindful and present, failing to see the other side of the coin, which entails what we need *to stop doing*. This is equally critical in avoiding the trap of perpetual dissatisfaction with life and the present.

Having books, a meditation practice, or other tools, without critically examining them within the contexts of our individual lives is like being shown how to build a house without being told that we need to live inside it to benefit from its shelter. Mindfulness is a tool, presence is the house we build with it, and the realization that we need to stop waiting allows us to finally go inside and sit by the fire.

"Not waiting" is an important stepping-stone on the path into the wild because time is observed differently in nature. You don't need to read Walden to understand how relatively important the concept of time is to our civilization, as compared to the wild. In nature, time passes. In civilization, time drives, gives significance, and dictates how we live. It's this time-centric perspective that gives birth to the concept of waiting. Animals allow time to pass, however they don't allow it to torture them. A bear finds the perfect moment to swat at a fish, a bird nests until it's time to migrate, and a spider sits silently as flies meander into its web. These actions are hunting, nesting, and sitting. To call them waiting would only make sense from our human perspective since animals are not suffering as a result of wanting to be elsewhere.

A Tale of Two Foreigners

I knew two U.S. Peace Corps volunteers in Senegal who lived in remote desert villages. They came from similar backgrounds and were each intelligent, kind, and pleasant to be around. Their respective communities each housed around two hundred residents, lacked access to utilities, and were located several hours from the nearest city by public transport. Each of the volunteers had a room in the house of a village chief and spent their time on similar agriculture-related projects. They were well-liked and only traveled outside their communities a few times each month. From the outside, it seemed the two were having fairly similar experiences.

However, to my surprise, the stories that each of them told before returning home after two years made it sound as if they had been on different planets. One volunteer had been quite content. She had enjoyed chatting with her host family at night, learning to cook local dishes, and attending community events such as weddings and baptisms. When she left the village for short trips, she was often equally happy to return home as she had been to get away. She felt she had learned a lot and was eager to take those lessons back to the United States as she continued her career.

The second volunteer was exhausted and agitated. He had liked his host family, although often only spent enough time with them to justify going off to read or sleep. He missed American food, comfortable beds, and air-conditioned rooms. His trips out of the village had gotten him through his two-year service and he often dreaded returning when they were over. While he didn't feel that anything was particularly wrong with his living situation, his village, or his family, he was constantly preoccupied by the existence of the more comfortable world from which he came and would one day return. With this on his mind, he found himself constantly waiting. Waiting for his next trip into the city, waiting to go visit his volunteer friends in other areas, waiting for his two years of service to end. He was stuck in this mindset of waiting, which led to a perpetual state of dissatisfaction. There was nothing overtly wrong with his situation; it simply wasn't where he wanted to be.

These two volunteers exemplify how strongly our mentalities can impact our perceptions, creating very different interpretations of similar experiences. The second volunteer, perhaps due to circumstances beyond anyone's control, lacked presence. This reduced the extent to which he benefited from, and was beneficial to, his community.

We only gain the capacity to give our present situation the attention and care that it needs once we stop longing to be in a different place or time. The second volunteer wasn't ready to give this level of attention. Unfortunately, when we're not ready, we often end up waiting until we are.

Waiting State of Mind

When we think of waiting, we imagine idly sitting at a bus stop or in a doctor's office. However, this only characterizes the "activity" of waiting, failing to capture the more damaging underlying waiting "state of mind."

Imagine it's Tuesday and you get a call from an old friend who wants meet up at a local restaurant on Friday. You're excited because you haven't seen them in years even though you used to be very close. Despite your excitement, you aren't about to go to the restaurant immediately and sit for three days in anticipation, so one could argue that you won't be waiting in its most conventional "activity" sense. However, your friend remains in the back of your mind that week as you go about your business. Maybe your mental preoccupation with the upcoming reunion makes you restless and distracted. Perhaps this restlessness leads you to duck out of work a few minutes early, skip a workout, or watch re-runs on television instead of starting a new book.

These things may happen because fixating on the future takes energy and effort. When we spend our energy thinking obsessively about the future (waiting) we reduce the amount of energy we can dedicate to the present. This means that even if we're not physically waiting, the mental state of waiting can still impact our lives. Even when we're *physically present*, we can be *mentally absent*. In light of this, it may be helpful to redefine our understanding of waiting to include "mental preoccupation," or waiting as a state of mind rather than a physical action. The real danger of this waiting is that we often don't even realize when it's happening.

Since we can be in a waiting state of mind while doing other things, it's also important to mention that we can be "doing nothing" without waiting at all. In a sense, this is mindfulness meditation, the practice of cultivating presence and awareness. We can even be physically waiting but not in a waiting state of mind, as long as we are content and present. Take for example a man sitting at a bus stop, listening to the birds chirp in the trees and watching pedestrians walk back and forth on the opposite side of the street. The bus arrives after twenty minutes, and he gets on having not "waited" for even a moment.

The idea that he was able to physically wait for the bus without "waiting" is important because the waiting state of mind is often more burdensome than the activity of waiting. Meditation can be one way to pull ourselves out of perpetual waiting and into the present, however it is not the only way. Simple understanding and recognition of waiting as it happens can also be enough to put an end to the cycle. The man at the bus stop may have recognized he was becoming anxious thinking about how long it would be until the bus arrived, deciding instead to observe the vibrancy of his surroundings. With that simple realization, he stopped waiting and began joyfully experiencing the present moment.

While waiting isn't absent from the animal kingdom, the perpetual waiting state of mind is far less prevalent. A friend recently pointed out to me that her cats wait for food each day, knowing when it will come and even purposefully arriving at their bowls early. While these animals engage in the activity of waiting, there's no indication that they allow a waiting state of mind to detract from their enjoyment of the rest of their lives. Like the man enjoying himself at the bus stop, animals remain present, even as they physically wait. When this waiting seems to bring them anxiety, we can also consider that they've been domesticated and are perhaps adopting a human practice that they too find unnatural.

Good Things Come…

It's often said: "good things come to those who wait." At its heart, this adage expresses that we must accept the natural passing of time and cast away our desires for immediacy. In other words, it tells us that forcing things prematurely will diminish their value.

While this is a noble sentiment, it could benefit from a slight rebranding, taking into consideration our understanding of waiting as a mental state rather than an activity. When we understand waiting as a mentality, we see the idea of waiting and the idea of time passing as separate. The former is the mindset we have while the latter happens. Therefore, there's no connection between "waiting" and "good things happening." Instead, the connection is between "good things" and the passing of time, regardless of whether that time was spent waiting or not. So, we can clarify that "good things come to those who allow an appropriate amount of time to pass between the present and an anticipated event." Catchy, I know.

Is this an important distinction or tiresome semantics? It's simply an example of how reflecting on concepts such as waiting can dramatically shift the meaning of truths that we often take for granted. Let's break down the adage just a little further by considering two scenarios. First, lets think about the effects of truly waiting for good things to come. Here, we'll likely fail to appreciate or maximize the potential of the time leading up to the anticipated good things since we'll be focusing only on the reward of our waiting. When those good things come, our orientation towards the future will make our enjoyment brief, after which we'll move on to waiting for the next reward. In this scenario, waiting may have brought good things but it also diminished each part of the experience. Conversely, if we're present while allowing time to pass, we can live fully in the time leading up to an anticipated event, enjoy it as it occurs, and continue to live presently after it is over. So perhaps we can conclude with a third version of the adage that is both accurate and simple by saying, "good things come to those who are present."

A swan will sit on its eggs for six weeks before they

hatch, present, protective, and attentive. It will show no visible signs of boredom, impatience, or discomfort. A person, taking a train home will get frustrated after twenty minutes of inactivity. Both the swan and the person have good things coming, and both must allow a given amount of time to pass, but only one of them will wait and only one of them will be anxious as a result.

Patience

We tend to assume patience is a tolerance for waiting. We believe a patient person is someone who is able to grit their teeth and suffer quietly. However, when we see "waiting" as a frustrated state of preoccupation with the future rather than an action, patience becomes never allowing ourselves to slip into a waiting mindset at all. Here, a patient person is someone who not only fully accepts that time must pass, but is able to enjoy that time as much as they will enjoy their anticipated future. Our goal shifts from being able to endure waiting to being present enough that we're not distracted by things to come.

Impatience is as much an effect of waiting as it is a cause. We experience waiting (fixating on the future) because we're impatient (frustrated with the present) and are impatient (frustrated with the present) because we wait (fixate on the future). As we live fully in each moment, we lessen our longing for future moments, accepting and appreciating the natural passing of time. So the *more patient we become*, the more present we become and *the less we wait*.

Perhaps waiting is so frustrating because the passing of time is one of the few things still completely out of our control. An unstoppable, immutable force that human kind has failed to master to even the smallest extent. Waiting is in many ways the punishment for that failure (or perhaps the punishment for the attempt). It makes us feel powerless as we sense time is passing too quickly or too slowly.

In neuroscience, it's been shown that having control over our environment is a neurologically satisfying condition. It's why we feel better unnecessarily carrying a sweater on a walk or over-packing our suitcase for a trip. We feel secure knowing that if our environment changes, we, as all-powerful humans, will be able to change it back. Unfortunately, unlike temperature, food availability, or any other environmental contingencies that humans have succeeded in mitigating the effects of, we remain helplessly at the mercy of passing time. This makes it one of the scariest concepts that modern, sheltered, and food secure humans must cope with. With this in mind, patience (and presence) also entails an acceptance of our powerlessness against time. Patience requires us to relinquish our desire for control and accept that some things are beyond our reach.

Conversely, we often think of "not waiting" as synonymous with impatience. However, when understanding waiting as a mindset, we see that these are actually opposite phenomena. "Not waiting" entails not fixating on the future, whereas impatience entails frustration due to a lack of presence. We generally fail to see this because when we conceptualize waiting as an action, "not waiting" equates to doing something immediately. Whereas, when seeing waiting as a mindset, "not waiting" means being present during the time before an anticipated event. In this way, people who do not wait cannot be impatient. It is only people who compulsively choose to wait by fixating on the future who become frustrated with their own waiting.

For our collective health, we may benefit from culturally redefining the significance of phrases such as "don't wait" that suggest waiting as an activity, to be ended by immediate action. These calls encourage us to reject the natural passing of time. The same phrase however could be a call to completely accept the natural passing of time. "Don't wait" could mean, "don't act immediately, but also don't spend your time wishing something would happen before it's meant to." This would require us to understand the necessity of time elapsing between events and focus on being present in each passing moment. With this, it becomes clear that impatience and not waiting are in fact complete opposites.

One undeniable difficulty of not waiting is that it requires us to appreciate, respect, and accept each present moment, even when they evoke negative emotions or reactions. When the present is difficult, we naturally want to devalue our experience, minimize its impact, and hope that it passes quickly. In these times, our perspective is narrowed as our focus is brought directly onto our suffering. We're overwhelmed, as our mind struggles to move elsewhere. We become confused and fatigued by the present, leading us to think about the past or fixate on the future. Such attempts at distraction not only prevent us from understanding our struggles but also lead to perpetual patterns of similar behavior.

When we respect each moment, we see its inherent value and refuse to sacrifice it. We allow ourselves to step back. To see the entire portrait of our existence, including both the dark and light. We begin to worry less about a sloppy brushstroke or a crooked line. We begin to realize that there's no point in finishing sooner or later. We begin to understand that we're the painter, not the painting, and that putting down a shadow can add as much beauty as a ray of light. No time is unappreciated. No time is wasted.

Realizing the value of the present can help lessen our desire to change the pace of passing time or fixate on the future (or past). This brings a contentment in knowing that future events will come as they will, bringing enjoyment or hardship, while present events are also experienced to their fullest. This is true patience.

Refusing to fixate on the future is also distinctly and importantly different from not being excited about the future. We can be excited without wishing for something to occur sooner. Excitement is a reactionary emotion that can be felt and enjoyed in the present. Waiting is a choice to remain outside of the present. We must honor our excitement with an appreciation for the fact that gratification will come in its own time. Please do not allow attempts at not waiting, to lessen any present feelings of joy or excitement.

The Speed of Time

When considering waiting as a state of mind characterized by discontent with the natural passing of time, we can separate periods of waiting into two modes:

1) *discontent with the present while wishing for a better future;*
2) *lessened contentment with the present out of fear of a worse future.*

Put more simply, these modes could be described as waiting for something relatively good to happen versus waiting for something relatively bad to happen. In terms of passing time, these modes could be described as time moving too slowly versus time moving too quickly. The former prevents one from enjoying the positive aspects of a perceived negative present, and the latter lessens the enjoyment of a positive present out of fear for a relatively negative future.

Both these forms of waiting reduce the significance we place on the present. They suggest that we're holding back on fully experiencing life until an anticipated future arrives. Dedicating this attention to the future means we are not fully immersed in our present lives.

This type of thinking is a trap. While a bus may eventually arrive, the future never will. Instead, we'll continue onward, never fully enjoying ourselves. When we run with our eyes fixed on the horizon, we can neither expect to reach it nor enjoy our immediate surroundings. As we get closer, the horizon moves further away and our surroundings continue to go unnoticed. Once the moment we're waiting for arrives, a new future moment will take its place and the waiting will begin again. Ultimately, it's up to us whether we choose to let waiting characterize our lives or enter our minds at all.

Regarding the second mode (anticipating the end of a positive experience), one may say, "just because I'm aware that good times will eventually end doesn't mean I don't enjoy them." This is absolutely true. While this type of waiting lessens our enjoyment of a positive experience, it doesn't imply that it will make our lives horrible or painful. It simply means that this type of waiting will add a layer of anxiety to an otherwise joyful time. Imagine for a moment that you're with someone you love. What emotions make that time special; comfort, belonging, ease, affection? Now imagine you're fixating only on the fact that the person will soon be returning to their distant home. How do you feel? Perhaps longing, fearful, or in dismay. Objectively, nothing in this situation has changed other than your perception. You've shifted from a present state of mind, which brought contentment, to a waiting state of mind, which brings anxiety. This exemplifies how waiting can occur just as easily while enjoying something pleasant (such as time with a loved one) as when suffering through something difficult.

In reality, most experiences aren't inherently negative or positive but are rather defined by the lens through which they're interpreted. This may explain why your spouse loves family camping trips while you suffer through them in misery. The camping trip alone has no emotional implication. It's the campers imposing their perspectives, predispositions, and personalities on the experience that transforms it. What we often fail to understand is the extent to which we have control over our perspectives, predispositions, and personalities, therefore maintaining the ability to construct our own realities. If we decide to be waiting through an experience that causes discomfort, then suffering will come to characterize that experience, even if it has the potential to bring joy. We determine our enjoyment of life and the only time we can stop waiting is now.

Determining Values

Perpetual waiting can also influence our values. When we experience something, we typically focus on the part of the experience that corresponds with what we value most. Say we go to a party with some friends. Afterwards, one friend may say, "It was great to see all those people again," whereas another may say, "the music was amazing." These two different individuals valued different parts of the same experience and used those values to build their narratives for understanding and retelling their stories.

When we're waiting our focus shifts from what is happening around us, to the future. This puts *the perceived speed at which time is passing* in the forefront of our minds, causing it to characterize and define an event. When we form our memory of an experience around the speed of passing time, we value time over other, potentially more important components. Imagine you stood in a slow line to buy movie tickets. The first thing you're likely to recount is how long you waited or how long the line was. Waiting made time a main focus and therefore a central value in your narrative. Choosing to recount how slow the wait was (aka the perceived speed at which time passed) demonstrates that time was valued over the beauty of the stars overhead or the frivolous conversation that took place behind you. These other components of the same experience hold the potential to bring great joy. Yet we diminish their importance unnecessarily.

Recently, a co-worker asked me how my winter holidays were and I found myself responding with a not uncommon refrain - "too short." Upon reflecting, I realized that my dread over a long upcoming business trip was putting me in a waiting mindset that had reduced my mental presence as I spent time off with my family. My response was evidence that my waiting led me to view my vacation in terms of passing time, reducing the extent to which I was able to focus on the many other more important values that had been part of the experience.

A mentality characterized by presence places value on the experience itself. If you're in the movie ticket line standing with presence, you may later describe the personality of the person you went with or the beauty of the theatre building rather than reporting on the length of the wait.

By making time a central value in experiences, we fundamentally change the metric through which we measure positivity or negativity. When waiting, our assessment of an experience exists on a scale from: 1 - relatively painless waiting, to 10 - horribly painful waiting. Regardless of where we fall on this scale, we've chosen to see the world through the inherently negative frame of waiting. If we see ourselves as "standing outside a theatre" (instead of waiting to buy tickets) then we may measure the experience on a scale from: 1 - the weather is a little rainy and my legs are tired, to 10 - it's a magical evening and I'm surrounded by passionate movie-lovers. Ultimately, it's not about where we fall on that scale from 1 to 10, but instead about what scale we decide to use.

Framing experiences in terms of waiting takes the insane complexity of the world and reduces it to the philosophical, man-made metric of time. It's like an economist measuring the value of a national park solely by its ability to generate revenue. While it is certainly a metric, it's one that completely misses the park's true value; just as characterizing my vacation as "too short" completely missed its true value.

So why is it so difficult to remain focused on meaningful values over passing time? One reason may be the way that our culture teaches us to value time. In the United States, we're constantly reminded that time is of the utmost importance. We hear that "time is money" and that "time flies" from a young age. It becomes the central pillar running through our lives, allowing us to orient ourselves and gauge our progress and self-worth. Have we spent our time well? Are we in the right place at the right time? How much time do we have left to accomplish our goals? However, in adopting this cultural value, we close a path to experiencing other hidden joys: the omnipresent, non-fleeting beauty that surrounds us. While we may not need to forget the existence of time all together, realigning our values to the extent that we no longer judge an experience based on how quickly time passes has the potential to bring about significant positive change in our lives and our world.

Animals in the wild never de-value the taste of a catch based on the length of the hunt, or disregard the warmth of a nest based on the duration of the build. As humans, we not only add these time-based metrics to our value systems, but make them central components, despite the fact that they predominately reduce our happiness (whether it be through stress, regret, or devaluation).

Life and Death

When we understand waiting to be a mindset, we can cease to associate it with any individual event that is "waited for," knowing that such an event won't satisfy the compulsive urge to be oriented towards the future. When we remain fixated on the future, we continually believe that whatever will come next will provide us with the happiness, satisfaction, and contentment we're looking for. However, when waiting, such satisfaction will always remain just around the next bend, until we reach the end of our lives. In this sense, living outside the present moment - waiting for a future event - is a practice of waiting for the final event: our death.

If we spend our lives futilely waiting for contentment to come, we'll feel resentment as we near life's end, not having achieved it. If we continuously find joy in the present, we may no longer see death as a darkness approaching, but rather as a light fading.

There are countless ways to conceptualize life and death, many of which give different value to the time we have on earth. Unfortunately, social stigma and fear often discourage us from thinking and talking explicitly and candidly about death. We're led to think it's too dark, too intense, or even too silly for normal conversation, despite its ability to significantly impact how we spend our lives and the extent to which we wait for them to end.

Those who obsessively fear death often diminish their enjoyment of life, just as waiting diminishes the enjoyment of any other experience. Accepting life as finite can be liberating. When we see death as a natural eventuality, we remove the stigma, fear, and dread associated with it. We diminish the almost magnetic energy that pulls our focus towards the future. Religions that de-stigmatize death through the existence of an afterlife or reincarnation can serve a similar affect, allowing many to peacefully confront their mortality. Valuing our remaining lives based on the amount of time that's left only brings anxiety. Therefore valuing each present moment is essential. It's the difference between rejecting and accepting mortality; the difference between wishing to never die and understanding death as a necessary part of life; the difference between perpetual waiting and presence.

The point in our lives at which we explicitly reflect on death can significantly impact when we're able to stop waiting and cultivate presence. If we only confront this reality late in life, we may feel bitter over the time we've lost, leading us to suffer greatly. We may feel too deeply engrained in the process of waiting for happiness to actually seize it. Conversely, approaching death may lead us to realize that there is nothing more to be waited for, forcing us to be present and appreciative.

People speak of personality changes that accompany aging, which often skew towards either enlightenment or intolerability. These changes may be reactions to the realization that there's nothing more to be waited for after an entire lifetime of waiting. We must try to understand this before reaching old age and find joy in the fact that much of life's beauty is made meaningful by its brevity.

When I find myself waiting or anxiously wishing for an experience to be over, I often think of my own death. I imagine myself on my deathbed or having recently died, and think about what I would give to experience that difficult moment once again. To feel the vibrancy, energy, stress, heat, love, joy, sadness, pain, and intensity present in each instant we're alive. This perspective can help us move through layers of difficulty and hardship to show the miracle that underlies each moment of consciousness.

WAITING

Thinking Ahead, Living Now

Similar to the nuance between waiting and excitement, there's an important difference between "not waiting" and "not thinking about the future." A common response to "live in the moment" is "well, I still need to think about my future." However, it's a misconception that these ideas are at odds with one another, since thinking about the future, planning for the future, and even predicting the future can be accomplished without wishing for it to come sooner. Living presently entails understanding the fact that the present moment is all that will ever exist. This doesn't require us to reject the fact that the future will someday be manifested as a present moment. We must plan for the future and work towards it. However, in doing this, we must not numb out the present with intense feelings of anticipation and desire.

The phrase, "live in the moment," isn't the same as saying, "think only about the moment." In the present, we can think about whatever we wish, including the future. Living in the moment simply means that we understand and accept our present reality while we engage in this planning. It means that we appreciate the present to the same extent that we plan to appreciate the future. We understand that rejecting the present in anticipation of the future will only lead us to reject the future in anticipation of a further future.

This reveals the fact that living in the moment isn't an activity (similar to how waiting isn't an activity). We can't simply choose to live in the moment for an afternoon by having a few drinks and forgetting about our worries. Living in the moment is a state of mind based on appreciation and awareness. It's a mentality of non-waiting, that once cultivated, becomes the perspective with which we see and think about all our experiences regardless of their immediacy.

Expectation

Since waiting describes a fixation on the future, it inevitably leads to the creation of hypothetical scenarios, mental visualizations, or fictional ideas of how upcoming experiences will go. We call these expectations. Since expectations evolve from a future orientation, they could be considered a by-product of waiting. We maintain these expectations despite the fact that we're seldom able to correctly predict the future.

Unfortunately, when we realize our expectations are inaccurate, we experience *cognitive dissonance*, or a discomfort caused by the inconsistency between our beliefs and experienced reality. This discomfort reduces our enjoyment of an experience. While it's natural to set and have expectations, it's also important to recognize that they rarely lead to healthy mindsets or positive emotions.

So what types of expectations exist? First, there are positive expectations. When these are unrealistically optimistic or "high," they can lead to disappointment. However, even when high expectations are accurate, they may still diminish our experience by removing the element of surprise or leading us to take it for granted. For example, imagine getting a sweater for Valentine's Day. If you expect to get an all-expense-paid vacation, you'll most likely feel negatively about the sweater. However, even if you expect to get a sweater, it will still bring far less joy than if you hadn't expected anything at all. Accurate expectations can turn a surprise into a requirement, needlessly reducing the impact of the gift or experience.

Now we can also consider the possibility that our positive expectations are set unrealistically low, so that the anticipated event exceeds them. Perhaps we expected to receive a bookmark, and we're overjoyed to have gotten a sweater instead. This may bring about relative joy; however, this joy is still only equal to the difference between our expectation and the actual outcome, which is less than it would have been had we had no expectation at all.

From an economic perspective, let's consider measuring our enjoyment on a numeric scale from -10 to 10. Positive experiences are represented by positive numbers and negative experiences by negative numbers. Zero represents our neutral state, implying no positivity or negativity. Now, say our expectation for a positive future event is 5. If the event occurs below a 5 we'll be disappointed. If the event occurs at 5 we'll be content, and if the event occurs above 5, say at 7, our marginal enjoyment will be 2. This 2, while positive, is still less than our marginal enjoyment had we had no expectation at all (in which case it would have been 7). This demonstrates that minimizing expectation not only hedges against potential disappointment but maximizes our capacity to enjoy the future.

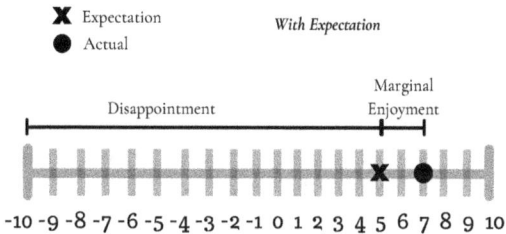

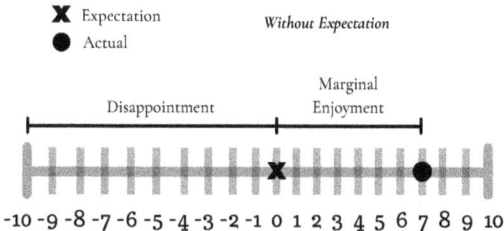

X Expectation
● Actual

With Expectation

Disappointment

Marginal Enjoyment

-10 -9 -8 -7 -6 -5 -4 -3 -2 -1 0 1 2 3 4 5 6 7 8 9 10

X Expectation
● Actual

Without Expectation

Disappointment

Marginal Enjoyment

-10 -9 -8 -7 -6 -5 -4 -3 -2 -1 0 1 2 3 4 5 6 7 8 9 10

So, why not have negative expectations for positive future experiences? If our goal is to maximize our marginal enjoyment wouldn't this allow us to turn that 7 into 10 or 15 (by expecting a -3 or -8)? Why not expect spiders for Valentine's Day so the sweater will be that much sweeter? Firstly, negative expectations slowly change the way we see our environment. When they're inaccurate, we risk negatively shifting our own perception. We may begin to resent our spider-giving significant other, despite the fact that they've only ever gifted us with comfortable sweaters. Secondly, negative expectations draw our attention, leading us to fixate on the future. This can bring us into a waiting mindset, which in turn causes us to further build our expectations, fueling a vicious cycle. Ultimately, if our goal is to maintain a mindset that allows us to have positive future experiences, neither negative nor positive expectations seem preferable to having no expectations at all.

Now let's consider how expectations influence inherently negative experiences. Say, for example, we need to have a difficult conversation with a co-worker about their lack of professionalism. We're dreading the confrontation and expect it to be unpleasant. Initially, we may say, "by having low expectations I am preparing myself for the unpleasantness, and if it isn't as bad as I expect, I'll be pleasantly surprised." This may be true, but we must also consider the effect of negative expectations on the time between now and the anticipated event. Just as with having a negative expectation for a positive experience, our negative expectation for this negative experience, even if accurate, will make us anxious and uncomfortable not only during the conversation but the entire time leading up to it. That discomfort will lead us to fixate on the future, bringing us into a state of waiting and diminishing our ability to enjoy the present. It brings part of our future discomfort into our present. If our anticipated event then turns out to be better than expected, we may also find ourselves resentfully asking, "why did I waste my energy all day, worrying over something like this?"

While low expectations are likely less damaging than high expectations, their ultimate underlying problem is that they still create a lack of presence. Saying "low expectations are better than high expectations" is a bit like saying "driving at 40 mph without a seatbelt is safer than driving at 60 mph without a seatbelt." It may be true, however the greater point is that it's still a dangerous behavior with little reward.

While the effects of expectation are too numerous to cover in detail, these examples demonstrate that expectations *do* change how we experience our lives. In most cases, unchecked expectations cause damage. We may suffer to different degrees depending on the specific situation and expectation, but most often we're left relatively worse off. Expectations also put us in a self-reinforcing waiting mindset. Waiting causes expectation and expectation leads to waiting, a circle that brings us out of the present and into a hypothetical future.

Theory and Practice

This brings us to the larger question of how we can practice living in the present. How do we move beyond our tendency to wait and fixate on the future? Countless religious leaders, gurus, consultants, and coaches have answered this through numerous techniques and approaches. However, I've often found jumping into practices such as mindfulness meditation to be difficult without first clarifying and understanding what exactly they are aiming to achieve. Simply thinking about mindfulness is a necessary precursor to finding the motivation needed to practice.

This helps us understand how and why mindfulness contributes to our happiness and contentment. It allows us to experientially understand the logic connecting mindfulness, presence, and peace in each of our lives. With this understanding, we can approach a mindfulness practice that is not dogmatic, but rather tailored to our individual needs. Our learned perspectives, viewpoints, teachings, and practices, must be tempered with a personal understanding of broader beliefs on life's meaning, joy, and purpose.

To me, mindfulness means not waiting and returning to the wild. To others, mindfulness may mean awareness and living with discipline. To another, it may mean seeing clearly and acting with compassion. These are different understandings of the same concept. The Buddha famously warned not to mistake a finger pointing to the moon as the moon itself. Individual interpretations are all different fingers and our experiential understanding of mindfulness is the moon. We can collect the practices, ideas, and philosophies of others, however, we will not be able to integrate them into our lives until we look up and see for ourselves. With this in mind, we can see how practices for cultivating mindfulness may differ from person to person depending on what makes sense to them, fits in their lives, and is compatible with their beliefs and objectives.

Two practices that have been helpful to me could be called prescriptive and preventative meditation (perhaps it's no coincidence that meditation sounds so similar to medication). As a prescriptive practice, we may take short breaks when we notice ourselves fixating strongly on the future or past. In these moments, we can remind ourselves of the risks these thoughts present to our psyche and mental well-being. We can review our understanding of mindfulness, at times taking notes or speaking out loud if it is helpful. Then, we begin tuning into our breath. Listening, watching, and experiencing deeply our environment. This will lead to the release of all thoughts and logic, allowing us to concentrate only on our sensory perceptions. We may then close our eyes and isolate each sense individually going deeper into the moment until nothing exists outside of our immediate surroundings. Through this, we enter an animalistic perception of the world. It moves beyond memory and metacognition. It plugs us into the living soul of our environment.

As a preventative approach, we may want to use physical activity to sustain a meditative state for relatively longer periods of time. We can choose an activity that presents some specific natural sensation that brings us deeper into the moment and into our environment. In yoga, the gentle movement of the body increases physical awareness. Walking through a forest or garden stimulates the visual and tactile senses. Whatever activity we choose, it is important that it increases our sense of connection to our surroundings. Our aim is to move away from the mind and into the body. The body cannot travel into the past or future as the mind easily does. It is always present, grounding us.

These practices are ways we can make our presence like our home. When living presently, we only casually glance at the past or future through windows while remaining rooted in our surroundings. This is a place where life is lived fully and felt deeply. When we lose our presence, we risk living on the other side of the window, trapped in the darkness of our fear, dissatisfaction, and nervous anticipation. From the outside, we can only see the warm fireplace through the glass, and only feel its heat through cracks in the walls.

We often see mindfulness and presence as niche interests. Ideas to ponder on a day off or rainy afternoon. But as we start to experientially understand their meaning and impact, it becomes clear that they are the very frameworks within which we experience our lives. They hold a profound ability to bring about substantive change. This is not a hobby. This is life.

PART TWO: CONNECTION

The Author and the Ants

There once was an author who lived in a suburb outside San Francisco. On one particularly sultry afternoon, he found himself sitting on a curb, sullenly staring at the small sprouts of grass peeking through cracks in the broken sidewalk. It was mid-day, and the sun angled awkwardly into his eyes, blocking his vision of the highway thirty feet ahead. He spit shamelessly, the saliva dangling from his lip for a brief moment before sluggishly dripping to the ground. Small beads of sweat formed shimmering jewels on his forehead, which he knew signaled the swamp that would soon form on his back and underarms. He glanced down at his phone, before remembering he already knew the time, having checked just minutes before.

The author pondered calling a cab, rather than continuing to wait for his friend, who was supposedly coming to pick him up. He even flipped through his address book and found a cab company, only to abandon the effort at the last moment, worrying that his ride may eventually arrive and be angry to find no one there.

His friend was a quiet man in his early thirties whose quick wit was only matched by his short temper. They had met at a writing seminar some years ago and bonded over testing one another's knowledge of 20th century existential philosophy. They would get drinks once a month to share their latest works and bounce new book ideas off one another, their ambitious personalities always assuring that their time together was purposeful and productive. So when the author's brakes had started to smoke and screech, forcing him to leave his car at the garage, he had figured that this relationship was close enough to merit asking for a ride home.

The author was popular, having achieved moderate success from his last several books. His contact list was full of names – agents, colleagues, publishers, and admirers – that he often failed to connect with faces. While the line between friends and fans sometimes seemed blurred, he received invitations to more social gatherings than he had the desire or energy to attend. Despite his ambivalence towards socializing, he greatly appreciated the idea of his popularity. Having grown up as a quiet child, he felt reaffirmed in his social development by the vast network he now maintained.

The author had dated several women in the past few years, some more seriously than others. He ended his most recent relationship around six months prior, recognizing that its passion had fizzled out over time. They had been almost casual as they parted ways. He appreciated the lack of drama, and she accepted that she didn't really know him well enough to feel wounded by the departure.

The secondary nature of this relationship was indicative of the author's true focus, which remained consistently on his writing. His books and articles symbolized his progression through life. They benchmarked his identity over time, leaving a lasting impression of his existence on the world. He believed that as they became more powerful, he became more powerful, and was convinced that when he reached his peak, his ideas would change the world.

Discussing ideas with his sea of acquaintances was

the author's most satisfying form of socialization. He made philosophical musings and intellectual challenges the centerpiece of any conversation, to the great amusement of admirers who often felt as though they were watching a performance while they were with him.

Yet despite this popularity, the author felt a familiar loneliness creep up from the depths of his subconscious as he sat on the hot curb waiting for his ride. He wondered if anyone who knew him truly cared that he was stranded in the heat, or if he got home safely, or if he was happy returning to his empty one-bedroom apartment at all. He scrolled through his contacts for someone to call, looking to distract himself from these unpleasant thoughts, but ultimately decided that any unprompted conversation would feel forced, potentially damaging his reputation.

He looked down to his right, searching for a different distraction and saw a line of ants scampering hurriedly down the sidewalk. They carried clippings of fallen foliage much larger than any of their tiny bodies.

"You guys wanna chat, or do you have to *leaf*?" he quipped, slightly disappointed by his own joke, then tried to redeem himself by adding, "Headed somewhere import-*ant*?"

The small creatures continued their march as the author stared intently. "Ants don't talk," he reminded himself, as the beads on his forehead began to coalesce and drop to the heated pavement.

His own words echoed in his head, turning into a song which he chanted under his breath.

Ants don't talk.

Ants don't talk.

Ants don't talk.

Yet as he looked at them, he could tell that despite their silence, they understood one another. They moved together, they lived together, and they worked together.

All he ever did was talk. He talked in his books, he

talked to his so-called friends, he was even talking to himself in that moment. Yet regardless of how well people understood what he said, he knew they didn't understand him. Regardless of his skill in communication, he knew he still lacked the ability to connect.

This nuance seemed lost on the ants, who survived through their natural connection to one another. Unlike the author, their pride was overshadowed by a common goal, and their individuality by their common experience. While the author's friends would read and listen to his ideas, they ultimately had very few commonalities. Furthermore, he knew nothing of their goals, motivations, or desires. He had learned so little of their lives, and remembered even less. Despite the care and wit with which he crafted his words, this one-way communication gave his relationships an air of superficiality that the ants mocked with their harmonious interdependence.

For a moment, he hated the tiny creatures, defensiveness rising like a wall to protect his delicate ego. They were slow, unaccomplished, and simple. They lived provincial lives, devoid of glamour, popularity, or prestige.

And still from behind that wall, he saw in them something he desired deeply. A lone tear slipped down his cheek to join the growing puddle of sweat on the pavement, so subtly that any onlooker would have simply seen a man sitting quietly in the sun.

An ant, however, may have noticed the subtle shift that occurred.

The author began to question his success, as waves of realization battered against rocks of anxiety within him. Were the metrics he used to gauge his accomplishment valid? Should he measure his life in books sold, reviews received, and contacts collected? Did he even feel truly successful, or was it just a label others had attached to him for so long that he internalized and adopted it?

His head snapped up as a voice pierced his shroud of contemplation. "Hey, are you coming?" His friend called out an open car window. He nodded, swinging open the door and stumbling into the sedan's bucket seat.

"Where you headed?" his friend asked.

"Just going home. Were you on your way somewhere?" the author replied.

"Grabbing some groceries. I can drop you at your place on the way to the store though."

"Mind if I tag along instead?" the author asked. His friend shrugged, nodding his head as they pulled away from the curb. Together, they merged into the long line of cars steadily moving together down the single-lane stretch of highway.

Communication for Connection

The year was 2003, and America Online Instant Messenger (AIM) was at its peak. This marked the beginning of the communication revolution that would take place in the coming years. There was a brave new frontier of online communication, the effects of which, both positive and negative, would fundamentally shape not only how we communicate but also how we relate to one another.

However, as an adolescent at the time, what I remember most about AIM wasn't the platform but rather the substance of the conversations it hosted. Despite the technology's novelty, the majority of conversations over AIM were anything but innovative.

A typical AIM conversation usually went like this:

Person 1: Yo ....(Hello)

Person 2: Yo, sup ………………………..(Hi, what's up)
Person 1: nm, u …………………………(Not much, and you?)
Person 2: jc …………………………………..(Just chilling)

Such conversations would generally happen after school, compensating for the long hour that had elapsed since having seen the other person. Yet, this made sense, because people weren't talking to convey information, but rather to connect.

Notably, this connection required a moderate level of effort. First, you had to boot-up and log into the computer, then dial-up to connect to the internet (blocking your regular home phone line), log-in to the AOL system (inputting your username and password each time), and actively scan for who was also online and could chat. This great effort for relatively meaningless conversation was evidence of how much connection was valued.

Today we've completely integrated technology into our everyday lives. The incredible ease with which we can communicate means that we no longer need to make such efforts to remain interpersonally connected. Yet somehow, it feels as though this lack of required effort leads us to take connection for granted. We now connect to communicate rather than communicating to connect. But…back to AIM.

On AIM, there was neither an urgent message to convey, nor a great problem to solve. Connectivity was the end goal, rather than the means. Years later, after seeing the novelty of technology fade, we've gone in the opposite direction. Instant communication is now as short and focused as possible. Connectivity is the means and communication the end goal. It's practical and goal-oriented. It's how we get things done, rather than how we occupy ourselves when there's nothing better to do. It's a way we can continue moving forward without being with one another, rather than a way to be with one another while we are physically apart.

Now of course, we still text socially and sometimes send messages with no purpose other than connection, but this is no longer the primary function of online communication. We've evolved to express ourselves in different ways, and use tools for different purposes. I highlight this evolution in communication to frame two simple questions, which we must ask ourselves.

Why do we communicate?

When does that communication allow us to really connect?

It's these questions that brought me to a second personal "communication revolution" over a decade later while living in Senegal. Senegalese culture and language emphasized several interesting communication norms that were new to me. Two of the most significant were:

Never pass by someone without acknowledging them. This could be as formal as "As-salamu alaykum," the international standard of acknowledgement in the Muslim world, or as simple as looking at someone sitting on the ground and stating, "you're sitting."

Never enter a room without greeting everyone. While this practice is common in many parts of the world, the Senegalese additionally require the ritualistic repetition of a string of pleasantries including; How is the family? How is the heat? How is the daily fatigue? How is the morning/afternoon/evening? And the list goes on. The answers to these questions aren't quite as important and could be as simple as "I'm here," or "thank god."

These practices each emphasize how crucial acknowledgement is in Senegalese culture, and by acknowledgement, I mean really seeing and accepting that the person standing in front of you is another human being.

While there are many more words in a Senegalese greeting than "sup" and "nm," the custom of greeting reminded me of my AIM conversations. Perhaps, because that was the last time I regularly communicated in a substantively meaningless yet powerfully connecting way; the last time I'd had a consistent practice of genuinely greeting and acknowledging. These types of conversations bring people together because they are interactions for the sake of interacting. They aren't difficult, they aren't complicated, they just say, "I care about you, so we're going to talk." That is communication for connection.

On a more recent work trip to Senegal, I saw a westerner in a fancy hotel yelling aggressively at a concierge over a minor problem with his room. To the guest's (and my) surprise, the concierge calmly looked back at him and stated, "I know this is a problem, but you need to respect me." It was a powerful cultural reminder of how we tend to forget that there are "people" involved in situations that we perceive to be "problems." A reminder that we must begin interactions with recognition and respect, regardless of the substantive issues that follow.

Researchers have found that thousands of animals around the world engage in turn-taking conversation purely for the sake of bonding and connection. Lemurs, for example, have been shown to engage in social vocal exchanges at a distance to build relationships with one another. They recognize that connection is important to their survival. What we need to appreciate as humans is that it's also important to ours.

Communicating to Connect

Reflecting on Senegalese norms, I began to wonder where in my adult life I'd lost this explicit practice of communicating to connect. I even felt distain towards excessive "small talk," and would critically judge social interaction that I saw as uninteresting or unproductive.

Was a conversation witty, unusual, or entertaining? Did the social connection benefit me in some way? Did it solve a problem or teach me something new? These were my metrics, and while they weren't incorrect or immoral, they didn't allow me to see the full potential of communication. Even when talking on the phone to close friends or family I would sometimes hear myself say, "well, I don't really have much more to tell," before wrapping up a conversation. Now I often linger through short pauses, appreciating the simple fact that such calls allow me to exist in the same space as my loved ones regardless of whether I'm across town, out-of-state, or halfway around the world.

Many of our beliefs concerning communication are cultural. Growing up, I learned that "good" communication was persuasive. It was clear, accurate, evidence-based, and impactful. As an undergraduate business student, I learned that "good" communication was efficient and effective (as everything in business should be). These lessons were correct. However, it's also correct to say that "good" communication is non-violent, familiar, caring, and empowering. It's correct to say that "good" communication is often non-verbal and typically non-judgmental. We can be excellent communicators with any of these values, yet our full potential rests in our ability to uncover and adopt them all. Valuing connection, I now *also* attempt to communicate genuinely, sensitively, and supportively, filling the gaps in my former cultural communication style.

I often used to quote Oscar Wilde, who said

"conversation about the weather is the last refuge of the unimaginative." It led me to avoid talking about weather for years. Now I'm of an opposite mind. While conversation about the weather may not be imaginative, productive, or even particularly interesting, it's a common language that allows us to connect with those around us when we may otherwise feel unable to.

In or Out

Connection has the critical power to unite and expand our social circles. However, when we don't communicate to connect, we often fail to see essential similarities between ourselves and others. This leads us to form social circles based on our unconscious associations, preferences, and predispositions, broadly called biases. Our biases lead us to accept only those with whom we share obvious similarities, while avoiding or rejecting those who are seemingly different. Intentionally connecting with and recognizing others on a human level helps us circumvent initial bias-based reactions, allowing our social circles to grow not only in size but also in diversity and inclusivity.

When unobserved, biases have the potential to reinforce strong social divides. They may lead us to push others away without even realizing it. However when brought into our awareness, biases can contribute to connection. Being aware of our subconscious preferences allows us to determine which are valid and which are illogically rooted in negative emotion such as fear or past trauma. Through understanding our reactive behavior and remaining open-minded, we begin to see previously unnoticed similarities between others and ourselves.

These similarities are essential since our minds tend to almost immediately sort new people into one of two categories. Those with whom we associate form our "in-group" and those with whom we don't form our "out-group." The similarities we share with our in-groups are often obvious. We see ourselves in them. They're trusted. They're friends. Our out-groups are harder for us to understand. We may share similarities with them, but those similarities are unclear or unseen. This obscurity leads to distrust, dislike, and often fear.

While lecturing on bias, a psychology professor at Columbia University once told us that the first three things people see are race, age, and gender. In a social world where we're making countless and constant comparisons, these three easily recognizable traits are the first filter through which we form our in- and out-groups. This isn't because they're the most important similarities, but rather because they're the most evident.

Unfortunately, once our initial judgments are made, it's increasingly hard to change our minds because we automatically begin to assume that one difference means there are numerous others. We believe that because someone looks differently, that they also think, behave, and feel differently.

This is another cognitive bias known as the halo effect, which suggests that we tend to take a single trait or limited assessment and assume it applies to all aspects of a person or situation. Most commonly, we discuss the halo effect in terms of positive or negative attributions. For example, when we see a well-dressed man, we're likely to assume he's also smart, kind, and trustworthy (a trick many con artists capitalize on). Or, when we meet someone with a short temper we assume they're also unkind and unfriendly.

However, the halo effect can also apply to perceptions of similarity and difference. When we see someone who is different in some small way, perhaps they're wearing a hijab in a Christian area or speaking with an unfamiliar accent, we're likely to expand that perception to assume that there are also other more significant differences. We assume that they don't enjoy our foods, don't understand our jokes, and don't share our hobbies and interests. Before we even begin thinking about these relationships in our conscious minds, our subconscious has already sabotaged them through bias and assumption.

This makes our unfamiliar out-groups increasingly unfamiliar and our assumptions about them increasingly negative. These beliefs are then reinforced by similar assumptions from other in-group members or negative messaging (on television, social media, etc.) produced by our in-groups. Slowly, the number of people we feel we can relate to shrinks. The world becomes scarier. Our lives become lonelier.

Intentionally fostering connection can stop this process. By acknowledging others or engaging in small-talk we can find simple ways to interact and uncover hidden similarities. This could be as easy as helping someone at the grocery store or chatting with a colleague that you usually avoid. Through such small efforts, with an awareness of bias, we can form far more diverse in-group affiliations.

Here's a quick exercise you can use to begin cultivating an awareness of bias. Grab a piece of paper and take no more than 2 minutes to write down the ten people you like most. Then take two more minutes and write down the ten people you trust most. Then continue to write down ten people that you dislike and ten that you distrust. Don't take too long to think about your lists and don't worry if names are repeated across categories.

When you're done write down your own race, age, and gender, then note the race, age, and gender of the names you listed. How many people that you like and trust are similar to you? Are there people that you trust, but don't like? Are there people that you like, but don't trust? How do you think similarities and biases play into each relationship?

Individual exercises like this can be helpful, because

we often need to reflect by ourselves before we feel prepared to discuss these sensitive personal issues with others. This enables us to observe our predispositions honestly, realistically, and without judgment so that we can accept bias as natural and normal. With this knowledge, we can compensate for irrational bias that may be injuring our relationships or preventing new members from entering our in-groups.

An awareness of bias opens our minds to seeing the hidden similarities that we share with others. These may include common experiences, abilities, desires, fears, inspirations, hobbies, areas of study, or forms of self-expression. We are so much more than our age, gender and race, yet we too often fail to appreciate our own incredible complexity.

Practically speaking, expanding our in-groups also directly impacts our behavior. Think for a moment about how you, idealistically, believe people should behave. Perhaps you're thinking: treating others as you'd like to be treated, giving people the benefit of a doubt, giving a smile and wave as you walk down the street, or lending a helping hand when you have some extra time. All these idealistic behaviors are, in fact, courtesies we typically extend only to our in-groups.

We favor them, we nurture them, we share with them, we emulate them. We act like the human beings we want to be, but only in their presence. When we think about who we are – our best selves – we're imagining who we are when we're around our in-groups. This means that our ability to be who we want, is intimately linked to how we see and accept the people we're around. The more people we push into our out-groups, the less often we behave as we believe we should. Accepting others makes us better people by our own standards.

Fear and Loathing

Just as fostering connection expands our in-groups, fear and hate reinforce the mistreatment of out-group members. This in turn creates more fear and hate. Jeff Greenberg, Sheldon Solomon, and Tom Pyszczynski present an interesting perspective on this phenomenon in what they call Terror Management Theory (TMT).

TMT tells us that as we're increasingly reminded of our mortality, we gravitate towards things that may continue our legacies beyond our death. In this context, *fear* is what reminds us of our mortality, and our *in-groups* are what we feel will carry on our legacies. By fear, I'm not only referring to imminent danger, but also the wariness towards change and the unknown that we all experience throughout our lives. The fear of being alone because we don't fit in, the fear of falling behind as our community changes, the fear of not having access to the resources we need, or of not being able to protect or provide for the ones we love. As we're reminded of these subtle, underlying fears in our daily lives, we're drawn closer into our in-groups, which in turn reinforces and feeds that same fear, drawing us closer in still.

Needless to say, this gravitation towards our in-groups impacts the level of distain, disregard, and even hate we show towards our out-groups. We're not just moving towards those we associate with, but away from those we don't know. With this said, it seems evident that making our in-groups as broad as possible would positively impact our lives. However, as you may suspect, this is easier said than done.

In-group formation is as much a psychological reaction as it is a choice. We not only need to make the explicit decision to behave differently, but also convince our reactive brains that we are, in fact, similar and connected to our out-groups. These mental gymnastics are the root of mantras that attempt to show the superiority of human similarities over tribal differences such as "we are all one" or "we are the world."

Connection, in a word, is the process through which we recondition that psychological reaction so we can strengthen, expand, and redefine our in-groups with acknowledgement, understanding, and curiosity. Forming connections, especially with unfamiliar people, whether it be through "meaningless" conversation or shared experience, allows us to see similarities with out-group members that may shift them into our in-groups.

It's important to highlight the psychological component of all this, because it's easy to become defensive when our prejudices are pointed out. Speaking in terms of in-groups and out-groups can help remove the stigma in these conversations. The ultimate goal here is to accept the natural tendencies (such as in-group formation and bias) that pull us apart, and then focus on the *other natural tendencies* (such as connection, cooperation, and understanding) that bring us together.

Herds of herbivore species in Zimbabwe including water buffalo and zebra spend longer periods of time at the watering hole when massive elephants are also around. They understand that despite their incredible differences in size and appearance, they're sharing the same resource, and can protect one another from shared threats such as lions. They've expanded their in-groups beyond differing sizes and behaviors, to ultimately include different species, all in pursuit of their survival and peaceful co-existence. As humans, we seek the separation and destruction not only of other species, but other races, cultures, and individuals. Not only out of rational fear, but out of insecurity and perceived superiority. Our destructive instinct goes beyond even that of lions, who hunt for their own survival. We act against others at the cost of our own communities, homes, and environment. We reduce the size of our in-groups to the detriment of everyone, including ourselves.

Luckily, as we take small steps towards expanding our in-groups, the effects begin to multiply. We become more adept at recognizing the similarities we share, reducing the innate fear of socializing in environments that we don't fully understand. This can have a profound impact since many of our negative relationships are caused by a lack of understanding and familiarity. Therefore, increasing our knowledge of others can reduce the extent to which we perceive our social relationships as adversarial. As we learn by reaching out on an individual level and forming small connections, we open up the path to completely transforming how we interact and affiliate.

Independence

We admire people with private pools and planes, who produce their own food, or own their own islands. These individuals are celebrated for their ability to function independently. However, independence can be a double-edged sword that, when not reflected upon, can work against our desire for meaningful connection. This is because mindless independence often equates to *separation*. We commonly use the word independence to mean not relying on or being relied on by others. So what does this imply?

Let's begin with the positive. To strive for independence is a survival mechanism. As we increase our independence, we increase the certainty with which we feel we will be able to fend and provide for ourselves. Cooperation is also a survival mechanism, and the two needn't be mutually exclusive, but we'll save that for later. As independent individuals, we reduce the extent to which others have control over our happiness and safety. This results in increased personal responsibility, efficacy, and ability.

The second edge of the sword is that blind

independence can work against community, romantic commitment, friendship, and other forms of meaningful interpersonal connection. As we increasingly see ourselves as separate, our relationships become more competitive, particularly when resources are scarce (whether those be physical resources such as food or intangible resources such as recognition or power). We begin to focus more intently on satisfying our own interests and fail to care for those of others, because we feel there is no link between their success and ours. However, as we reduce our reliance on others and minimize the number of people relying on us, our in-groups shrink. Refusing to look outwardly is refusing to look deeply at the individuals around us. This reduces our opportunities to see those crucial hidden similarities that build community.

So, independence, while important, must be pursued carefully. As we seek to increase our own security, we must do it in ways that don't harm or detract from the lives of those around us. As we seek to be responsible for ourselves, we must also take responsibility for our roles in the lives of others. As we hone our abilities, we must practice them in ways that build connection and benefit community.

Community

Reflecting on the delicate relationship between independence and community is essential to finding a healthy balance between the two. Community refers to the collections of individuals that exist in the various social spaces we frequent. This could include both those we perceive as in-group and out-group members.

The first step towards balancing independence and community is realizing that complete independence is a myth. We are all active participants in massive interdependent social systems that meet our needs and desires – providing food, shelter, entertainment, education, etc. These systems, comprised of numerous individuals, groups, and institutions, enable us to function in modern society. In addition to social systems, our interactions, relationships, and experiences (all dependent on others) shape our lives and self-image. So believing that we're disconnected, self-made, or truly self-reliant is simply a refusal to recognize the larger reality; that our world, inevitably and infinitely extends beyond our individuality.

Once we move beyond the notion that total independence is possible or desirable we can shift our focus towards cultivating the positive effects associated with independence while also honoring our interconnectedness. Our goal can move from trying to be better individuals in isolation, towards trying to be better individuals within groups. We can begin thinking critically about what aspects of self-reliance are necessary and when we should rely on others.

Think about completing a group project at work. While we, as independent individuals, may be able to complete the project ourselves, sacrificing control and distributing portions amongst the group is likely to both yield better results, and foster a more productive team. This does not mean that individuals aren't independently responsible. It simply appreciates that the project is larger than any individual contribution. Life is also a big group project.

This understanding requires us to temper our search for self-reliance with a little uncertainty. Distributing responsibility and control is difficult, but necessary to build strong relationships and close communities. This could be called *reliance with others* (meaning relying on and being relied on). When we rely *with*, we build trust. When we build trust, we feel secure, open, and collaborative. For some, relying with may entail contributing to a community garden or potluck dinner. For others, it may mean being a member of a military unit or fire department. What's important is that we feel able to distribute trust and build community by connecting.

Even a small shift in perspective towards balancing our independence with interdependence can open the door to a larger shift in how we view the impacts of our actions on others. When we understand that we're inevitably part of a bigger picture, we realize that none of our actions exist in isolation. We begin to wonder how far the effects of our behaviors reach and whether our daily actions truly align with our beliefs.

Suppose we order a sandwich online. Do we think only about what type of sandwich we would like, or do we extend our thoughts to whether or not our family or roommates are also hungry? Do we consider whether or not the delivery company is treating its workers fairly, or whether the farm providing the ingredients is operating responsibly? Do we understand that by taking any small action, we become a cog in a large machine? Do we appreciate that as a cog, we are partially responsible for both the problems and solutions that machine creates?

The answers to these questions are influenced by how far our feelings of connection and community extend. Simply put, feeling part of a community, whether it be a family or global network, makes us feel as though the world is about more than just our own well-being. This feeling is integrated into the decisions we make in a million different ways, each reflecting our feelings of empathy and connection to others.

Self-Interest

As we distribute trust within our community, our personal interests are expanded to encompass our community's interests. This raises two interesting questions. How strong does one's sense of community have to be in order for one to act against their own self-interest, and when will the personal sacrifices required by community interests become too burdensome?

While important, these questions operate on the false assumption that self-interest is static and unchanging. They assume that as we adopt a community-oriented mindset, we will maintain our previous self-interests. In a way, it's indicative of how deeply entrenched individualist mentalities are in our thinking. A sense of community is not something that is at odds with self-interest because it redefines how we think of self-interest. Truly adopting a community means we adopt the community's interests as our own.

For example, our loved ones make up one of our closest communities. When we make sacrifices for those we love, we may lose something of value (money, time, opportunity) yet we rarely see it as against our self-interest because their well-being is integral to ours. Belonging to a community means that to some extent, the community's well-being becomes a priority.

The Giant Pacific octopus guards her eggs continuously for six straight months, carefully cleaning and providing them with oxygen, after which she immediately dies. Such a laborious process ending in death can hardly be considered a product of self-interest. However, it's not exactly martyrdom either. It's a demonstration of how much she values her eggs, who are in a sense, her community. Their interests are her interests, and her resulting death, which humans may consider an extreme act of self-sacrifice, is rather a simple natural continuation of the community.

Adopting community means adapting and reconciling our self-interests with those of the group. Those redefined self-interests then guide our actions. So, while community-supporting actions may be difficult, they are still a manifestation of our individual interests, transformed through our connections to those around us.

Dependent Individualists

Knowing that complete independence is neither realistic nor ideal, we can attempt to gain a nuanced understanding of the partial independence that allows us to engage positively with our communities. To do this, we will define independence as *the extent to which we rely on the external world to meet our needs*.

This definition is important in avoiding the common pitfall of considering independence to mean only financial independence, prioritizing the idea of not relying on *other people* for *money*. This fails to account for the fact that money is far from our only need, and other people are not the only thing on which we can rely.

When we focus exclusively on financial independence, we consider independent people as those who can afford to be taken *care of*, rather than those who can *care for* (themselves and others). In reality, these individuals are often equally as dependent on their caretakers (whether they be cleaners, restaurants, or drivers) as those who depend on their community, government, or family. The difference isn't their level of independence, but rather the mechanisms supporting them. Mistaking wealth for independence only makes us increasingly helpless as we slowly lose the ability to cook for ourselves, clean for ourselves, groom ourselves, transport and navigate for ourselves, and entertain ourselves. We both celebrate and sacrifice our independence simultaneously, becoming heavily reliant on the massive industries and systems supporting us.

Realizing that we're all *inter*dependent tells us that claims of independence are often actually expressions of individualist values. Such claims don't necessarily express a level of reliance but rather a value for the individual over the collective. This nuance shows that we can have both very *self-sufficient, capable collectivists* who recognize and leverage their interdependencies, and *dependent individualists* who deny their interdependences while promoting self-interest.

For example, let's contrast a fictitious high school teacher and a wealthy real estate investor. The teacher has just started her first job and relies heavily on her co-workers to help her understand the school environment. She discusses school policy as she carpools each morning with her vice-principal and uses her breaks in the teachers' lounge to learn from her colleagues' experience. Simultaneously, she cooks and cares for herself, maintains the school garden, and provides valuable expertise to the school community. She is both part of a *collective*, while also *self-sufficient* and *capable*. The investor, on the other hand, has the financial means to separate herself from society. She lives alone in a large home, is transported by a fleet of private cars, and only interacts socially with those wealthy enough to afford membership in her exclusive country club. This separation reinforces *individualist* values, leading her to consistently act in self-interest. Her expertise is focused on accumulating wealth and building her portfolio. When she needs to have something fixed, she calls her assistant; when she needs to eat, she calls for delivery; when she needs her clothes cleaned, she calls her maid; when she needs to exercise, she calls her trainer. While not relying on others for financial support, she is highly *dependent* on the staff that cares for her. To an outside observer, both of these individuals could be painted with the same brush – as independent. The teacher is bravely venturing into a new environment and the investor's wealth makes her beholden to no one. However, upon closer examination, we can see the critical differences between them. The former is a self-sufficient collectivist and the latter, a dependent individualist.

Dependent individualism, at its worst, means tacitly refusing to take responsibility for the well-being of those around us. Luckily, connection can be a tool against this.

In addition to expanding in-groups, connection builds empathy, which allows us to see and understand the feelings of others. When we do this, our interdependencies become clearer, showing us how we contribute to both human suffering and positive change.

Connection leads us to place value in our communities and take responsibility for their health and well-being. This can transform us from being individualists, overly dependent on commercial solutions to simple problems, into self-sufficient community members. Community and connection must both be considered a part of self-sufficiency because they are necessities to our individual mental well-being and health. We need them for our survival and happiness.

The lines between individualism, collectivism, independence, self-sufficiency and reliance are blurry. They should be. Sharp separations and universal truths are typically asserted for the sake of argument rather than understanding. To understand, we instead need to see that these are simply words we use to describe complex and overlapping sentiments. As individuals, we can exist within collectives and within communities. Similarly, it is our position in our community that allows us to maintain our individuality. Self-sufficiency allows us to productively and meaningfully rely on others without being overly burdensome. Simultaneously, understanding our inevitable dependence on others means that we must realistically consider the ways in which we take care of ourselves through connection. We must rely on, show gratitude towards, and reciprocate those who enable our survival. There is no lone individual nor is there an absolute community; no one lives in a vacuum, nor does anyone sacrifice all personal responsibility. The challenge we face is to understand the complexity of these ideas and their unique implications so that we can begin to use this new understanding as motivation to connect, grow, and come together.

Showing Up and Hanging Out

We know that connecting is important, however it's often easier said than done. Building relationships with new people requires us to put ourselves out there and show vulnerability. This is challenging.

So how exactly do we connect? We can start by relating back to the idea of presence. Presence forms the bedrock on which connection is built, since to connect, we must be present in a shared space (whether it be physical, virtual, mental, or emotional). This space creates one of the most basic similarities that can exist between any two individuals, allowing them to relate to one another. Think of a time that you've connected with someone outside of your typical in-group. Was there a shared space that facilitated the interaction? Would that connection have been possible had you lacked presence or been mentally preoccupied?

I recently found myself in a long line at an airport in Guinea. My plane was delayed and the passengers were getting increasingly agitated. To cut the tension, I struck up a conversation with a nearby police officer. Despite our apparent differences, we ended up chatting for thirty minutes and both left feeling not only calmer, but more connected to one another. Our interaction was possible because we both shared and were actively present in the airport environment – listening, looking, and exploring. In a crowd of agitated passengers, staring intently into their phones or gazing longingly out the windows, we maintained our presence, and were able to recognize one another because of it. In contrast, once I boarded the plane, I put on my headphones and went deeply into my own mental space. While there was a man my age, with whom I shared multiple apparent similarities sitting in the seat next to me, we made absolutely no connection. In this instance, we shared space yet I lacked presence. These contrasting experiences demonstrate that both shared space and presence are crucial factors in our ability to connect to others.

We often justify negative relationships by saying that we don't "have anything in common" or "share similar interests" with those we've failed to connect to. These are valid barriers with which we all struggle. However, we often overlook the ways we can connect aside from shared qualities or experiences. Presence has been one of the most effective and surprising ways that I have encountered, particularly when communicating across cultural and language barriers.

Through years of living in homes in Europe and Africa, with families from diverse cultures, speaking only foreign languages, I've learned one thing: "good" conversation, while enjoyable and important, always comes second to simply being present, whether that means sitting around the house, helping with mundane tasks, or tagging along on a casual evening out.

In my most meaningful relationships, what's changed me from houseguest to family member hasn't been wit or charm, but rather the consistency with which I sat in the living room reading, watching TV, and co-existing.

It's almost as though an environment, whether it be a house, a class, or a neighborhood café, is a living organism. When you pass by occasionally, you're like a hat or glove. You'll be enjoyed, perhaps provide some warmth or maybe even an annoying itch, but ultimately, you'll be taken off and put away. When you're consistently present, you become a part of the organism, whether it be a hand, a mind, or a heart. You help define what that space is and how it affects those within it. When you're part of something, you never really leave, because a piece of you will always remain in the character of the space itself.

You could think of the effect of presence on a relationship as pushing a needle on a spectrum between "stranger" and "family" (with "friend" being somewhere in the middle). When we're not present, the needle gets pushed further and further to the left until the relationship simply ceases to exist. When we're mildly present, we're often judged on each experience we have. If we have a great time, people may say we're great. If we're annoying, we'll be judged accordingly. This is because those limited interactions are all others have to go on. This could be called the friend-zone. When we're fully present, that is to say a permanent fixture, we're no longer judged on each small action, because those around us have a breadth of experiences with us that contribute to their complex understanding of our individuality. Better yet, we are accepted for better or worse as part of the territory we inhabit. This is the space of family. The people we love but don't choose.

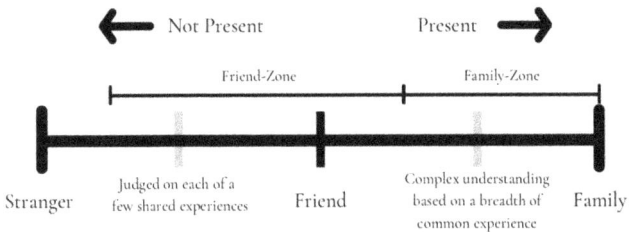

I expect that many of us already experientially know and understand this spectrum. Yet, we still so often wonder, strive, and suffer endlessly to push that needle in one direction or the other without realizing the important role of simple presence. So when we're struggling to integrate into a community, become a family member, or simply maintain a close connection, instead of overthinking and overanalyzing, remember: *the first (and often most important) step is simply showing up and hanging out.*

Connecting Honestly

Honesty is a second foundational component to connection. When honesty is absent, our actions aren't truly reflective of our beliefs or values. Therefore, the connections we make are not our own, but rather those of a fictional character we've created and are playing. In essence, when we're dishonest, we temporarily become other people. This doesn't mean we aren't responsible for our actions, but rather that the people we relate to through those actions cannot truly see, understand, or connect to us.

Such a lack of ingenuity may result from our attempts to fit into a group, impress a romantic partner, get a job, or any number of situations in which we feel compelled to behave like others. These are strategic lies we tell to become more amenable to those around us. Unfortunately, the longer we walk around in the skin of these characters, the harder it is to get back into our own. This can be especially harmful when our characters act against our principles, since we're prone to internalize patterns of action. We must be honest about who we are, so that we can maintain our ability to express ourselves and form genuine relationships.

In addition to being honest about who we are, we need to be honest about the state of our relationships. This means being able to express how we truly feel about those around us (both positively and negatively). When we can't express appreciation to those we love, we risk losing them, and when we can't critically evaluate poor relationships, we risk letting them pull us down.

Failing to honestly evaluate the negative effects of an emotionally harmful friendship not only deteriorates any potential positive elements of the relationship but breeds contempt. Recognizing such effects and openly discussing them is a type of honesty that facilitates adaptation, ultimately strengthening and repairing the connection. Failing to honestly communicate negative feelings to a romantic partner may lead to excessive fighting or hidden distrust. Conversely, honest communication and expressions of concern may allow emotions to be addressed while appreciating the underlying love that still exists. We all know that no relationship or connection is perfect. Yet, despite this, we rarely openly act to address these imperfections, often to our own detriment.

Animals seldom hide such feelings. That ingenuity is likely a part of why humans are so attracted to them. We see the love of our animal companions as sincere and whole-hearted. We yearn for such direct, genuine connection despite our concurrent fear of it. The strength and mutual loyalty that comes out of these dynamics is spectacular. The lengths to which people will go for their animals, and animals for their people, is what we should aspire to with one another. Realizing the power of honesty and ingenuity in relationships brings us one step closer to building strong, meaningful, and personal connections.

PART THREE: ADVENTURE

Distant Family and Deep-Water Fish

There were once two fishermen, a sister and brother, who lived with their family in a small village. They took pride and pleasure in rising early each morning and casting their nets throughout the day, always catching enough to easily meet their needs. Inside their family home lived their mother, an adopted adolescent sister, and the brother's wife with her infant twins. While the family had grown over the years, little changed. The siblings had lived their entire lives in the village, never having traveled further than they could walk in any direction before sunset and never having made a true voyage to see the outside world.

Since no transport came to their community, visitors were rare. When they did come, the siblings would crane their necks to eavesdrop on their tales of adventure. While they appreciated their provincial lives, and loved their family, these moments brought feelings of yearning for something more; for a great voyage beyond the borders of the village, across the desert to the east or the ocean to the west. Alas, knowing they had no wealth and were relied on by their family, they were sure that these dreams would remain just that.

Early one morning, a strange man came to the

village. He wore heavy clothing and spoke a broken form of their language that the siblings struggled to understand. They had never seen such a man before, yet he spent several days eating, drinking, and chatting with their neighbors as if he were an old acquaintance.

One evening, to the sibling's surprise, the stranger walked casually into their small compound where they sat resting.

"Can we help you find something?" The sister, who was the elder of the two, asked earnestly. The man smiled, shaking his head. He explained that he was the grandson of a village elder who left a half-century ago, accompanied by the sibling's distant uncle. While he was visiting to reconnect with his own estranged family, he had also been asked to deliver a message.

The fishermen's father, having died when they were children, had told them little of his brother. Their impressions of the man were made only through the occasional story, told in passing by neighbors. According to the stranger, he had been working in a far away city his entire life, and had accumulated enough wealth to live in modest comfort.

However, as they say, distance makes the heart grow fonder. For their uncle, getting older as a foreigner to the city led him to realize how much he missed his family and childhood home. While he was too old to travel great distances, he wanted to invite his brother's children to visit, reconnect, and experience the fruits of his success.

The man reached out and handed the siblings two tickets. "If you like, you may return with me," he said matter-of-factly. "We will travel east for two days, until we hit the road, then follow it another half day to a large town. From there we can take a train directly to your uncle. It's a long journey, but he'll greet you with open arms and provide you all the amenities you need upon arrival."

ADVENTURE

The siblings looked at each other in shock. The moment they had been waiting for had arrived, an opportunity for adventure that would show them the outside world. However, as quickly as their excitement arose, their eyes fell back to their loving family, calmly waiting behind them having not understood the majority of the stranger's broken words. The siblings knew that they could not both leave, for there would be no one left to provide for and protect them.

The brother turned to his elder sister. "I'm young and have more time to see the world. You've taken care of me my whole life, taught me to fish, and always made sure I was safe. Please go and see our uncle. I will stay here and make sure the family remains well," he said.

The sister looked back down at him caringly and replied. "No, you're young and may find new opportunity in the city. I am already set in my ways here as a fisherman and would benefit less from such a voyage. I insist, you must go see our uncle."

They paused for a moment in silence. The brother knew that once his sister spoke there was no further argument to be made. So, at first light, he set off with the stranger, one man plodding along wearily towards the comfort of home and the other eagerly setting out in search of adventure.

The journey felt easier than the brother had expected. His village had given them more than enough food and drink to last their voyage, so they were able to trade some of the excess for the occasional ride on a traveling trader's donkey-drawn cart. At the town, the stranger booked them a night in a local inn. The beds felt unusually soft to the brother, and the novelty of electricity allowed them to stay up late chatting about his uncle as well as the stranger's own family. They caught their train early the next morning, and the brother watched out the window as the familiar stretches of desert turned to crowded markets and cement buildings.

At the station, the two quickly found their waiting car, which drove through the winding city streets until finally arriving at their destination. The stranger remained in the car as the brother got out, then waved goodbye through the window as he pulled away. The brother was left standing outside a house five times larger than that of his village's chief.

He paused for a moment, wondering if the location was correct, until his uncle suddenly burst through the front door with open arms. "Where is your sister?" he asked, with a hint of concern.

"She had to stay home to care for our family," the fisherman replied. Without further questioning, the uncle shrugged and ushered him inside.

As the days passed, the two ate delicious meals prepared by the uncle's servants and informed one another of the happenings in their lives. The brother laughed at the oddity of the urban world, and the uncle enjoyed the warm company of family, which he had so sorely missed. The stranger had spoken true when he promised that everything the brother needed would be provided. With his uncle, he needn't work for his food, nor worry for his safety, nor cater to his dependents. It was truly a vacation – perhaps the first he'd ever taken.

However, after several weeks, these comforts began to lose their novelty and the two exhausted the topics they felt able to discuss with one another. The fisherman began to miss his family more each day, until finally he announced that he was ready to return home to the village. His uncle, while disappointed, understood, wishing his nephew a safe journey home as he handed him a return ticket and food for the voyage. The journey home proved as easy as the one there, and the brother soon reached the village, finding his family's warm embrace. He told them stories of his travels, and just as he had eagerly listened to the tales of visitors in the past, they now attentively listened to his experiences.

The next day, the sister rose to go fishing. She could tell her brother was tired from his travel and happily set out alone so that he could rest and spend time with his wife and children. She was grateful that her brother had enjoyed his experience, although inevitably felt disappointed that she had missed her own chance for adventure.

This pang of lost opportunity inspired her to seek out a new fishing spot that morning. She had heard of a lake several hours to the west that few from her village visited due to stories of travelers getting lost on the unmarked route. Butterflies began to congregate in her stomach as she contemplated searching for it. She swallowed hard, silencing them as she decided to set out, secretly delighting in the challenge ahead.

About an hour into her journey, the sister felt an unusual wind at her back. Looking up and into the gale, she saw an immense wall of sand approaching from the east. The winds, having traveled thousands of miles, were carrying with them dirt and debris from across the continent, a phenomenon that, while not unheard of, only occurred once or twice a year in the region. While she had experienced these winds before, she had never found herself so far from a safe shelter when they arrived. Frantically, the sister scanned the horizon as the storm loomed overhead. There was nothing in sight but sparse shrubbery being blown almost flat to the ground as if an invisible boot had descended from the heavens crushing everything in its earthly path. With little recourse, the sister crouched low to the ground, threw her cape overhead, and sat on its edges to prevent sand from entering.

Debris bounced painfully off her back as the storm's intensity increased. Distracted by the discomfort, the sister barely noticed as water began to pool around her feet. She knew that the region's numerous lakes made it prone to flash flooding when powerful storms shifted the area's topology. This meant that the low ravine she found herself in could quickly fill with water. Throwing caution to the wind, she wrapped her cape around her face and scrambled up the nearest hill. She fell to her knees at the top, struggling to remain covered, until just as quickly as it had come, the storm disappeared, rumbling off into the distance. By the time the sand cleared from her eyes, the sky was blue and the wall of debris was no longer in sight.

The sister stood up and looked around, vigorously dusting off her clothes. To her surprise, the storm had changed the shapes and sizes of the surrounding hills, covering some bushes and uncovering others. It was mid-day, and the sun was directly overhead. For a moment, she panicked, realizing she no longer knew in which direction to travel.

She sat for a moment, partly out of fatigue, partly out of defeat. Her mind raced through possibilities of wandering until the evening hours, returning without food, or passing out from dehydration in the mid-day heat.

As reality set in, a small bird caught her eye. She recognized the species as foreign, knowing she would only see them migrating in the summer months. They would fly overhead in the opposite direction as she walked home with her evening catch. Knowing her village was east of her usual fishing spot, she deduced that the birds must fly to the west as the seasons change. Excitedly, she rose, now knowing how to return to her path.

As expected, a little over an hour later the edges of the lake came into view. The sister approached it, overjoyed, drinking deeply from the freshwater at its shores and bathing quickly to remove the dust and sand from the storm before wading into the deeper waters to fish.

She cast her net for several hours, as she had

thousands of times in her usual lake, yet despite her persistence, caught nothing. The sister was shocked. She had been sure the lake would produce a bountiful catch, since so few frequented its waters. She looked back to the shore in exasperation, wondering if it would be smarter to simply cut her losses and return home.

Just as she was about to give up, the sister noticed another peculiar breeze. She flinched at the thought of a second storm, but saw that it was the wind bouncing off the hills in a counterclockwise motion then sweeping down in circles over the lake. She could see this circular movement reflected in the surface water. She thought for a moment, before realizing that this unusual wind was directing the fish in a path that ran parallel to her net, allowing them to avoid her completely. Eagerly wading out further, the sister cast her net at a new angle.

Lo and behold, a bountiful school of rather large perch quickly swam into her trap. She heaved the net over her shoulder, pulling the massive catch out of the water and hauling it towards the shore. A smile swept across her face as she walked towards bank and sat to rest next to the awkwardly flopping creatures.

However, as she sat, her smile slowly began to fade. While her net was full, this was still a far reach from her brother's adventure. Her mind returned to the question of whether she would ever be able to seize such an opportunity.

Suddenly, the silence was broken by a small voice. A perch, having escaped her net, was now laying near her hand as it consolingly called out.

"Normally, you humans look happier when you capture and carry us away," it said. The sister blinked hard, wondering if the sun had affected her more than she had realized.

"I've caught a million fish," she replied, "what I want is an adventure." The fish thought for a moment, flopping gently.

"When you live in a small lake, you realize that running around in circles on the surface gets quite boring. We find adventure not by going far, but by exploring the depths," it replied.

The sister looked at the lake, pondering how deep its murky waters truly went. When she looked back down for the escaped fish, it was gone. Slightly shaken and aware of the late hour, she tied up her catch, and set off for the village.

As she returned to her family's compound, she pulled her brother aside, and told him about the day. She told him of how she survived the sandstorm, and warned that in such a situation, it is important to avoid low ground that can flood; she told him about the birds, and how they can help to navigate in unfamiliar environments; she told him about the wind and how it can affect the flow of the water making fish difficult to catch. Lastly, she told him about the perch that had spoken to her, its words both kind and cryptic.

Her brother sat quietly, listening to the story as if it were a great epic, entranced by the obstacles she had overcome. After several moments of silence, he slowly responded. "I think I understand what the perch meant."

The sister was shocked. "What do you mean? Certainly, it was a delusion brought on by the heat," she retorted.

"I've traveled a great distance with the comforts of good food, safe shelter, and pleasant company. I've seen a far away land with novelties and oddities, all of which were fun to discuss and remark on. I've met a new relative with whom I shared pleasantries and enjoyable conversation. Yet, I've returned still wondering if what I experienced was an adventure.

You've traveled a relatively short distance, but encountered life-threatening challenges, which you overcame and learned from. You've experienced great discomfort, which allowed you to earn a fantastic bounty. You've met a bizarre character that encouraged you to reflect deeply on your experience. Perhaps what the perch meant was that adventure is not found in the novelty of an experience, but rather in the challenge that it presents and the growth that it affords. For this, you need not travel far, but rather deep into your own desires, fears, limitations, and abilities. Knowing this, I think it may have been you who had the adventure after all."

The sister sat, pensively staring at the basket of fish in the corner. The next day, she took her younger brother to the far lake and they fished it together for hours. On that day, neither wished for any experience other than the exact one that they were sharing.

The Illusive Itch

When we think about our needs, our minds easily go to the basics of food and shelter. However, psychologists such as Abraham Maslow have encouraged us to reflect further by considering less tangible concepts such as belonging, esteem, and lastly, self-actualization. This final and most abstract need is the need to fulfill one's potential and find meaning in life. Unfortunately, this is highly conceptual, frustratingly vague, and nearly unattainable. How can we achieve a potential that we can't define? How can we find meaning in life, when such meaning continues to change as we grow?

These questions suggest that practically approaching the need for fulfillment in life requires a new frame of mind based on the idea that complete fulfillment is an illusion. As we reach our potential it expands. As we find meaning, it shifts. Therefore, the "need" in this regard isn't to satisfy but to pursue. We don't need to (or rather cannot) attain self-actualization. Instead, our true obligation is to endlessly strive for it.

That process of pursuit is what we call adventure, the messy road that brings us significance, meaning, and perspective.

This road is unique to each of us and will often lead in dramatically different directions. However, for most, it starts with an itch. An ambiguous desire for something more, different, and perhaps even a little dangerous. This isn't inherently good or evil, but rather a natural, raw motivation to act and live. It gives voice to the part of us that longs to push our boundaries. This same voice allows us to define our full potential both as human beings and wild animals.

While we can't assume to understand the motivations of animals nor the extent to which they pursue what we consider "meaning," we can admire the decidedness and commitment with which they approach the unknown, whether that be the surety of the birds that migrate across the world each year or the confident naivety of a dog, aimlessly wandering in search of new smells.

Humans commonly fail to leave their comfort zones with such resolve. Our anxieties, fears, and imaginations prevent us, even when we know that a step out into the unknown is healthy and beneficial. Like our animal counterparts, we must learn to walk down the road of adventure without hesitation, adopting their confidence and demeanor as we too, return to the wild.

Effort and Reward

During my time in Senegal, I would intermittently travel from my home in the northern border town of Richard Toll, to the old Colonial capital of Saint Louis, where I could meet friends and get a change of pace from my daily work with local entrepreneurs. It was a relatively quick hour and a half ride, stuffed in the back of a modified Peugeot with six other passengers. I would usually end up cramped against the window listening to music and watching the miles of desert stretch out in every direction.

After hopping off on the side of the road outside the city, it would be another half-hour walk to a communal apartment frequented by travelers in the region. From there, it was a quick trip to the hole-in-the-wall shop where $2 dollar gin and whisky bottles stood on a makeshift wooden shelf stewarded by the inattentive wife of the proprietor. A half hour and a few CFA Francs later, I'd be reunited with a motley crew of disheveled compatriots, carrying a box of snacks from the local gas station.

The eight of us would pile into a cab and direct the driver towards "the end of town, where the fisherman dock" in search of an abandoned stretch of beach on the Mauritanian boarder. We'd get dropped near a row of colorfully hand-painted boats and walk off into what seemed like a mix between a dump, a shipping yard, and a shanty-town. After weaving through workers, circumventing a makeshift graveyard, and nervously passing by a border-police check point, we would arrive at a magnificent hidden world, a stretch of beach nestled between the organized chaos of the city and the vast desert to the north.

Heavy tides created a steep shelf 50 feet into the ocean, causing shallow waters to extend unusually far off the beach, giving the impression of a gently shifting pond. Tides breaking over the island caused a strong, invisible downward current that washed away the usual trash and debris leaving the beach pristine. At certain times of year, a massive migration of small white butterflies would drift down the coast, passing just overhead, while the occasional smuggler on an over-loaded motorbike sped by. We'd set up a shade structure with a surfboard and spend the day drinking and swimming until the sun began to set and the local youth descended for their nightly football games.

I appreciate those times differently now. In my mind, the memories are clear, clean, and simple. However, I often forget the significant level of challenge and discomfort inherent to those trips. Firstly, knowledge of the existence and location of the beach was something that required a familiarity achievable only through living in the area, which meant not having hot water, limited electricity, a poor diet, and frequent (albeit benign) harassment. Then there was actually getting to the beach, which required long periods in awkward positions, constant sweating, and walking along shifting sands with heavy bottles and boxes. The sun was relentless, which explained the lack of inhabitants during the day, and our general lack of sleep and nourishment cast its own shade over our mental states.

None of this is to say that we didn't love Senegal, our work, or its remarkable people. Instead, it's simply to point out that certain hardships are often necessary to create truly remarkable experiences. Each challenge on the path of adventure precipitates into a droplet of meaning that gives life purpose. These circumstances were our path, and that view of the ocean from the beach illuminated the meaning behind it.

To me, this characterized an adventure. It required work, time, and discomfort, in addition to a degree of risk. However, these efforts paid off with an experience that reminded us why we were alive. An ephemeral beauty that came not only from the aesthetic of our surroundings but the combination of emotions, mentalities, company, and perceptions that were unique to those exact moments. It taught us that beauty, ingenuity, honesty, originality, and visceral experience were not only possible, but attainable, by taking us out of our jaded mentalities and into a world that felt simple and pure. It taught us that authentic experience exists for those willing to put in the necessary effort. These lessons helped us grow as individuals, shaping our understanding of how we could seek happiness and fulfillment as our lives went on.

This intersection of difficulty, risk, and reward is the heart of adventure, the benefits of which cut deep into our philosophical and practical understanding of how we should live our lives.

Difficulty and Challenge

If our need for adventure is that ever-shifting itch that motivates us to find meaning, our challenge becomes learning how to effectively scratch it. This starts by creatively seeking experiences that allow growth.

Unfortunately, we often seek to satisfy our desire for adventure with an increased quantity of the familiar. We attempt to address our feelings of restlessness by tiring ourselves out. We may take on more responsibility at work, intensify our exercise regime, or increase our use of alcohol. This often increases the stress and pressure that led to our lack of fulfillment in the first place.

We see a need for qualitative change, but only feel empowered to change the quantity of what we already know and do. This leaves us not only unsatisfied but exhausted. While we may have taken an important step forward in recognizing our desire for adventure, we also must learn where and how to find it.

This highlights the idea that things can be difficult without being challenging. Difficulty implies that a certain level of experience or skill is needed. To take on extra work responsibilities, we need sufficient experience to assure our managers that we'll be successful; to increase the intensity of an exercise regime, we must already have attained a certain level of physical fitness. In contrast, a challenge implies going outside our comfort zones. This often requires creative thinking and can be approached by anyone. For example, asking someone out on a date is often uncomfortable, but doesn't require a specific skill. Instead, it can be done in a multitude of completely different ways. Difficulty is progressive (linear, familiar, and cumulative), whereas challenge is creative and approachable from many angles and levels of experience. When we fail at something that is solely too difficult, we're often discouraged, whereas when we fail a challenge we often learn. Adventure is ideally both difficult and challenging.

For me, working while in grad school was difficult. It required long hours and sent me home exhausted each day. However, it was ultimately an application of skills rather than an acquisition. I was applying a formula – research, write, email, repeat. My academic work, on the other hand, felt like a challenge. It brought me into contact with unfamiliar topics and tools, and allowed me to experience negotiations and mediations through which I could learn. It brought about a similar exhaustion, however also allowed growth and generated excitement. This felt like far more of an adventure and was far more satisfying.

Many people find themselves in unfortunately difficult situations, overworked and under-stimulated. If we face that dissatisfaction by increasing the familiar, we must remain aware that we're increasing difficulty without addressing our need for challenge. Piling on activities, even when fun, may not provide the fulfillment we're looking for. Seek challenge that's uplifting. This will bring growth, realization, and the elusive feeling of purpose.

Reverse Engineering Adventure

While adventure is different for each individual, its effects are often similar. It motivates, inspires, gives new perspective, and brings about personal growth. So to understand what constitutes an adventure, we can reflect on times we've felt these effects, then reverse engineer the experiences that caused them. We may remember the feeling of finishing a race, standing up for a friend, or speaking at a large event. Feeling the significance of these occasions, we may realize that the bravery they required and lessons they taught exemplified adventurous experiences. We can then think about why those situations challenged us and how we can pursue such challenges again.

We can ask: Where is my comfort zone? How do I normally operate in my everyday life? What has recently challenged my preconceptions? How can I stretch, push, and test my own boundaries? Finding answers to these questions is like searching for a knot in a muscle. We feel around, attentively and cautiously to better understand our problem. Then we apply focused and firm pressure through the pursuit of new experiences that release our restlessness and tension.

Take social anxiety for example, a common challenge that requires significant attention to overcome. Questioning ourselves, we may see that our anxiety is based on a fear of being inappropriate or unaccepted. With this knowledge, we can push ourselves. We can find a safe space to have structured interaction, where there are simple rules that guide and facilitate conversation. Community pottery classes, book clubs and other events where people unite around a shared interest often offer such environments. Through these experiences we can gently push ourselves to forge new friendships and feel secure while socializing. While less obvious than bushwhacking through the Amazon, this process of challenge and growth is a great adventure. We simply must feel able and willing to find for ourselves.

For a perpetual city-dweller, backpacking in the mountains may have a similar effect. We may feel challenged by a fear of the unknown, motivated to

FERAL

experience the natural world, and inspired by a desire to connect with the environment. Approaching this challenge will then allow us to learn outdoor skills and discover new things about ourselves. Conversely, for someone who spends a lot of time outdoors, it may be more of an adventure to visit a crowded city. These very different experiences can have the same effect, depending on where we, as individuals, start. We'll readily find adventure if we remember that it's this effect that we're looking for, rather than a specific activity or experience.

The Yin and Yang

While we typically think of adventure in a positive light, we must also recognize that it often has negative, challenging, and burdensome components. Although it can be enjoyable, adventure is not synonymous with fun. Its purpose stretches beyond recreation, to encompass learning and growth.

Challenging components are essential to adventure because they indicate that we've left our comfort zones. This dangerous territory is where we are forced to adapt and learn, but also where we risk being hurt.

In my early twenties, I wasn't particularly comfortable talking to women. Pushing through my fears, I once made a very public declaration of love for a girl that I liked at a university event. There had been a raffle to celebrate the end of a mentorship program in which I'd participated, and I submitted an embarrassing nickname for my crush instead of my own. When it was picked, I was prompted to go up and explain what it meant in front of my whole class. She never spoke to me again. Even now, I cringe as I think back on that moment. Yet it forced me to confront my own fear and taught me a lesson in self-expression.

Adventure requires us a to roll the dice, meaning

from time to time, we're bound to lose. Yet we still need to enter that dangerous territory because *the unknown*, by definition, *is everything we have left to learn*, and the real possibility of failure gives that learning significance. Adventure is nuanced, a delicate balance of light and darkness. It goes beyond a vacation, necessitating an emotional investment, requiring us to take a leap of faith and commit to an experience.

The Wolf Science Center in Ernstbrunn, Austria performed a study in 2016 which demonstrated an interesting difference between wolves and domesticated species of dog. They gave each group a choice between two bowls; the first "safe" bowl consistently contained a dry food pellet and the second "risky" bowl either contained a piece of meat or a rock. What they found was that the wolves were far more likely to take the risky option (80% of the time) than the dogs (58% of the time). They concluded that the shift towards domestication made the dogs more risk-averse. While avoiding risk can be an important survival mechanism, we as domesticated humans often become too risk-averse. We fail to see that our need for fulfillment requires a certain level of risk and adventure, and therefore sacrifice our psychological well-being for our physical and emotional safety.

Commercial Solutions

The need for adventure - the desire for challenge and change - is a form of internal conflict. Luckily, conflict, when productively managed, is a means of creating positive change and transformation. We may be in conflict with ourselves around our rate of personal growth, level of achievement, or exposure to the unusual. We may be in conflict with our place in the status quo or the repetitiveness of our daily life. Conflict implies tension, and that itch for adventure is simply a tension, waiting to be unwound.

However, we're often encouraged to distract ourselves from our tensions and internal conflict. We are inundated with advertisements for goods and services meant to draw our attention away. We're fed short moments of satisfaction at a premium, in lieu of resolving our underlying need for self-actualization.

Each year, I visit an old friend in New York. When we get together, he consistently tells tales of his dissatisfaction. He hates his job, he feels alone, and he's tired. He even looks visibly pale, as though accompanied by a constant low-grade nausea. Yet, as we discuss these difficulties, his justifications repeatedly return to the fact that he's financially comfortable, stocked with the latest amenities and electronics, and active in the local bar scene. Ultimately, he feels powerless to bring about change because he only considers external, consumer solutions to his problems, despite the fact that they never seem to work. He feels he is doing everything he can.

His situation demonstrates the very relatable tendency we have to distract ourselves with material goods and commercial experiences. We look for raises when we need job satisfaction, for new clothes when we need confidence, and for drunken nights out when we need genuine friendship and love. We have these tendencies because we face pervasive advertising every day that is explicitly trying to communicate one thing; how *a product or service* can improve our lives. Unfortunately, as we increasingly accept the ways in which products improve our lives, we stop thinking about how *we* can improve our lives.

Resolving our internal tension with consumer behavior makes us less likely to seek out adventure or take risks to address our psychological needs. It tells us that comfort, ease, and consumption are our answers, when in fact, our self-actualization hinges on our ability to express ourselves, confront challenges, and overcome discomfort. Consumerism counterbalances the fear of the unknown with an assuring predictability. As we slowly buy in to this mentality, we lose our capacity to live adventurously.

In his book *Tribe*, Sebastian Junger notes that incapacitated mental patients in England during the Blitz suddenly rose from their beds to drive ambulances and help those around them. The need of the situation allowed them to meet their challenge. In our modern world, we are the mental patients. Emotionally incapacitated by our own culture, as it slowly removes the adventure from our lives. While less immediate than bombs dropping overhead, we must recognize this as a crisis and rise to the challenge of becoming functional, self-guided human beings. We must boldly confront the need for meaning in our lives despite the distractions working against us.

In the wild, when a fox needs food, it hunts, when a bird needs a mate, it calls out, when a bear needs to rest, it finds a cave to settle down. These are simple processes of recognizing needs and addressing them. In civilization, even when we recognize our needs, we often fail to address them. When we need food, we're presented with manufactured options of varying qualities and prices and are told by numerous competing companies that each of their products are the best. When we need companionship, we're presented with online catalogues in phone applications and on websites of other humans sorted by age and gender. Then we're told that only one person is right for us and that each platform is uniquely able to find them. When we need rest we're presented with infinite entertainment options that force us to weigh our desire for sleep against our desire for distraction. Then we're encouraged through advertisements that promote "binge-watching" and similar practices to ignore our health.

Our society complicates the most simple and basic needs, pushing us into positions where we feel incapable of addressing them. When we feel the need for adventure, the need to do something meaningful, we should approach it like a fox or bear. Through simple recognition and pursuit.

Attaching Value

The fact that consumerism won't fulfill our need for self-actualization, doesn't mean that physical goods can't have meaning or value. That value, however, isn't dictated by the nature of an item itself, but rather by the significance we attach to it.

One means of attaching significance is representation. This is when an item represents or serves as a reminder of something precious whether it be a treasured memory or loved one. Buying one hundred t-shirts online will never bring the same satisfaction as wearing one that was bought with a close friend during a memorable trip. Buying expensive jewelry will never bring the same satisfaction as wearing a simple ring or token of love from a significant other. This is because these objects contain in them *experiences and relationships* that address fundamental needs. The shirt reminds us of a treasured memory, and the ring reminds us of our love for another. The intangible value of these items far exceeds any market price.

A second means of attaching significance is through expression. This occurs when possessions reflect values that we hold central to our identity such as creativity, compassion, or respect. We may own bright clothes to express that we value levity or dress formally to show respect to our coworkers. In these instances, our possessions are still only given value by the internal characteristics they represent.

When we understand that our values and experiences provide underlying meaning to our possessions, then we see that all possessions are simply symbolic. If, through self-reflection, we realize that we value our personal growth vis-à-vis our career, a fancy car may be meaningful, but only as a representation of that growth and success. When we are led to believe that possessions have meaning, but we're unable to connect them to our own individual, underlying values and beliefs, then we fall into the trap of consumerism. Our attempts at satisfaction become like shoveling snow into the ocean: needlessly exhausting.

We then become easily confused by marketers and salesmen. We may value athleticism and therefore be led to buy clothing marketed by professional athletes instead of learning to play a sport. We may value adventure and therefore be led to buy cars that make us look daring instead of actually leaving our comfort zones. Failing to think explicitly about our underlying values leads us to seek empty representations of them. If you value athleticism, a headband won in a basketball tournament should be more valuable than a signature jersey. If you value adventure, the junker you lived in while driving cross-country should be more valuable than a flashy sports car. Heavily advertised commercial goods sell a narrative and lifestyle that we crave in our pursuit of meaning. However, they don't actually give us that lifestyle, and therefore they don't actually give us that sense of purpose and meaning. In this way, they're not nearly as valuable as they claim to be.

If we want to become golfers, we should spend more time on the golf course. If we want to feel daring, we should take a calculated risk, perhaps something we've hesitated to do. It's important to recognize that while possessions have their place, consumerism, most often isn't the solution. We must look deeply into the underlying values and needs that we're attempting to address through consumption, then use that knowledge to shift our behavior towards the pursuit of meaningful experience.

Linking the Short to the Long-Term

So, how is adventure so easily overlooked or unintentionally forgone? One explanation may involve the time frames we use when we set goals and objectives for ourselves throughout our lives. While most people have both short (up to ten years) and long-term goals, we tend to think short-term when we concretely plan activities and undertakings.

This short-term orientation focuses on making marginal advancements, whether they're in our careers, personal interests, or social lives. We think about what we can immediately *do* to move *forward*. We may want to finish a degree, become a senior manager, make ten new friends, or start attending advanced yoga classes. These goals are tangible. We favor them because we can see almost exactly what success looks like. We're motivated by the fact that they're concrete and attainable.

However for many of us, these goals change when our orientation shifts to the long-term. In this time frame, we consider more "state of being" oriented visions such as having a family, being well-traveled, being famous, or simply being happy. Interestingly, longer-term goals are often more centered around meaningful experience than relative advancement. The significance of having a family isn't in the action of having a child, but rather in the experience of growing and being with them; the significance of happiness isn't in the action of saying "I'm happy" but rather in its implication on our everyday lives.

Oddly, these two orientations give us two different sets of goals. Yet we concentrate so intently on the former, that we rarely consider how it will lead to the latter. When we get too caught up in the short-term, becoming focused on things we can immediately do, we limit our ability to think about who we want to "be." Less tangible, long-term goals need to be pursued immediately and constantly. Their impact on our behavior is like a wind, slowly shifting the landscape of our lives so that we, like a river, can flow in the direction we desire. We may not always notice the light breeze in the background, but if it ceases to blow, we'll end up flowing in the wrong direction.

Adventure combines short and long-term orientations. While comprised of short-term actions, the overall effect of adventure is on our long-term state of being. It creates immediate, yet intangible, value such as personal growth, perspective, and learning. If we wish to reach our long-term state of being oriented goals, we must make space for ourselves to pursue such experiences.

For example, if we have the long-term goal of being a kind person, we may need to engage in adventures that build empathy. This could mean anything from spending time with people from different backgrounds, to working with local political groups or volunteering at shelters. These activities broaden our perspective and challenge us to make diverse connections. Although they may not always feel as though they're "getting us ahead" in the short-term, they *must* be undertaken for the formative experience they provide.

In the long-term, it is far easier to see how the benefits of adventure are both concrete and desirable. We may only see the effect and value of sitting through a rainy, week-long camping trip in Appalachia years later when we realize that it made us braver and allowed us to overcome our fear of isolation. While it may not have earned us a badge, certificate, or recognition, its subtle effects helped to shape who we became later in life. Our choice to pursue or forgo adventurous experiences therefore depends greatly on our ability to stop thinking only of short-term rewards.

Seeing that an experience aligns with our values (our "being"-oriented long-term goals) must be a sufficient reason to pursue it. If we can chase these adventures, without hesitation, repeatedly and energetically, then like a dog chasing its tail, we may be lucky enough to end up happily tired with the knowledge that there's no place other than where we began.

Travel

Travel has always been closely linked to the idea of adventure. However, there is a new form of modern travel, which removes adventure from the equation. As the familiarity and ease with which we move around the world increases, the need for travelers to genuinely explore decreases. Travel packages promise "adventure" to exotic places at little cost and almost no effort. This maintains only the façade of adventure, removing any need for adaptation, navigation, or learning.

Take for example, luxury commercial expeditions up Mount Everest in which climbers are required to have little experience while they enjoy heated tents and gourmet meals. Contrast this with expeditions before the 1990s, when mountaineers needed years of experience and worked alongside local guides rather than blindly relying on them. While this example is rather extreme, even backpacking around Europe or the United States can now be almost completely orchestrated from a laptop prior to departure.

This convenience, while a blessing in so many ways, requires us to sacrifice a level of uncertainty that characterized adventurous voyages in the past. Such uncertainty allowed for many difficult but rewarding experiences. While it may be unrealistic (or undesirable) to completely forsake technology, we can still look for ways to find some balance between ease and adventure.

Furthermore, we need to consider the fact that this new form of travel has spurred the creation of tourist infrastructure that's often harmful to local populations and ecosystems. We must ask ourselves, are the ways we're traveling benefiting or hurting the areas we're traveling to? Is the tourist infrastructure in our destination built responsibly? Are we behaving in accordance with local traditions and customs? When we fail to consider these questions, we inadvertently destroy the environment, dilute local culture, and take advantage of marginalized, voiceless groups. Simultaneously, we fail to find meaningful adventure for ourselves. Whether it's the increased cost of living for locals spurred by the tourist economy in Marrakesh, environmental damage caused by large hotel chains in Bali, or the degradation and pollution of historical sites such as Machu Picchu, the negative effects of irresponsible tourism are abundant.

Actors in the tourism industry are quick to offer adventure through travel, because put simply, it sells. Unfortunately, they often lead travelers through superficial experiences with no need to meaningfully interact with local people, care for the environment, navigate the terrain, experience culture, or respect tradition.

This ultimately shifts the focus of our travel towards consumption. We cruise to small islands so we can drink on heavily polluting ships, fly to China to purchase knock-off Gucci bags, or visit South Africa to stay in large European hotel chains. Curators of these experiences sell comfort, in lieu of more interesting and challenging endeavors.

With this in mind, we need to rethink how we travel and match this to the type of experience we are looking for. We need to fully understand what constitutes adventure in our individual lives so we can curate our own experiences accordingly. We may want to search for authenticity, difference, beauty, or things that capture the essence of our destination.

A second challenge to remaining adventurous is,

ironically, the frequency with which many now travel. In my office at the United Nations, staff returning from international missions would always bring back small gifts. They would visit Africa, the Middle East, Asia, and Europe, sometimes working in cities and others times in remote areas. Despite this, their gifts would always be one of three different varieties of chocolate, bought in an international airport. Now, perhaps this was simply because the office staff were an afterthought on their long trip home (not a problem). Nevertheless, it signaled how habitual and mundane their travel had become.

It's easy to understand how quickly we can become jaded by strenuous travel and how destinations we initially feel are exotic can quickly become normalized. This is particularly true while traveling on business, when we take little time to appreciate the uniqueness of our destination and often have no energy to seek recreational challenges. Unfortunately, when we adopt this mindset we lose part of the magic that exists in the world. We unknowingly stop appreciating the great gift of the experience that's been given to us. Our fatigued and jaded minds increasingly gravitate towards the familiar and comfortable, made readily available by the travel industry, which presents us with an easy "out" at a high price.

So, remain adventurous. Maintain fresh eyes when viewing the world. Travel purposefully, and be mindful of heavily curated experiences that trade authenticity for ease, if authenticity is in fact what you seek. This way, we can rightfully preserve the historical link between travel and adventure.

Adventure and Presence

The nature of adventure and its contribution to long-term state-of-being goals implies that its value is in having an experience, rather than any immediate by-product. The benefit of spending a day exploring beachside caves may not be something as quantifiable as a map of the cave structures or photos of stalactites, but instead something intangible such as an experiential understanding of exploration. Since such experiential value always occurs in the now, adventure inherently requires presence.

Appreciating an experience for its own sake requires us to be mindful and aware. We're forced to forsake any excessive preoccupation with the future or we risk failing to fully experience our immediate surroundings. For this reason, adventure automatically pulls many away from their daily hyper-focus on results.

Cultivating presence through adventure can also serve to encourage spontaneity. Spontaneity arises when we're able to make decisions and take actions based on our immediate needs and observations. Recognizing these actions requires us to be closely in touch with our surroundings. When present, we can benefit from the self-reinforcing circle of *adventure* leading to *presence* causing *spontaneity* inciting more *adventure*, and onward.

When a cat saunters off into the woods, it's not thinking of how much weight it will lose during the walk or how its bravery will be judged by others in the cat community. It's thinking only about the shiny light it just saw or the curious noises faintly drifting into its ear. The cat is in the moment. It moves into the unknown for the sake of the experience, open to changing its mind, or setting out in another direction.

Adventure and Freedom

Like presence, the concept of freedom is embedded within adventure. This is because the existence of freedom creates the physical, mental, and emotional space that's needed to take risks and seek out new experiences.

In order to realize our adventurous aspirations, we need time, options, and creativity. We must feel empowered, spontaneous, and committed to our beliefs. These qualities are all present when we don't feel physically constricted by our surroundings, emotionally constricted by our relationships, or trapped within our roles. When we lack freedom, we feel unable to leave our comfort zones, even when we have the desire.

Physical barriers, such as a lack of transportation may prevent us from adventuring into the world. Work-related barriers such as only having experience in a specific field may prevent us from adventuring into new professional realms. Emotional barriers such as feelings of inadequacy may prevent us from feeling able to approach new challenges. When these roadblocks restrict our freedom, we lose our will to explore, inhibiting our growth and reducing the adventure in our lives. As you read this final section on freedom, keep in mind the ways in which all these concepts are interconnected. They are different perspectives on the same idea. Different signs, all pointing down the same path.

PART FOUR: FREEDOM

The Caged Accountant

There was once a girl who grew up in a quiet suburb with two caring parents who always made her feel as though she could do anything in the world. As a child, she would run around the living room pretending she was a falcon, since after all, her possibilities were limitless.

As a teenager, she learned to play the violin and in a short time became the first chair in her school orchestra. After high school, she went to a top-tier university to study accounting. She had a natural talent with numbers and easily secured a job at a coveted firm after graduation. In her free time, she continued playing the violin, now able to recite exquisitely complex concertos with ease.

One Saturday afternoon when she was twenty-seven, she met a man in a cafe near her house. They began dating and after a few years moved in with one another, then got married after several more. The man wasn't a particularly good listener and tended to remain emotionally distant, but he clearly cared for her and that made her happy.

Together, they enjoyed the next several years. Rising early, going to work, and returning home to one another in the evenings, all so they could wake up the next day and do it again. It was a blissfully simple ritual.

However, as time went on, this repetitive simplicity lost its appeal. The woman grew restless. Her work began to feel increasingly tiresome, as she spent her long days combing through spreadsheets and writing reports. She became exhausted by the never ending slew of mathematical puzzles she had once found mysterious and intriguing. The woman considered moving to a different firm, but feared she would spend her time integrating into a new organization just to end up doing the same job. So instead, she started a garden on her back porch, an easy but welcome disruption to her tedium.

Unfortunately, the space was small and could only hold a few plants. She would still pick up her violin from time to time, however had stopped learning new pieces. She now played the same songs over and over until the notes sounded stale and contrived.

After one particularly hard day at work, the woman decided to get a drink at a bar near her office. She was sitting alone, slowly sipping a whisky and soda, when a handsome young man approached and asked to buy her a drink. They talked for five minutes before she began to feel guilty, although she knew she had little reason to. Nevertheless, she excused herself abruptly, returning home to water her tiny garden.

Several months passed before her husband noticed her unhappiness. While his first impulse was to help, he had no idea how. So when he saw an exotic bird in the window of a local aviculturist while walking home one evening, he felt as though it was a sign – the perfect gift to lift his wife's spirits.

He brought the bird home and was happy to see his wife enjoying the company of her new friend. While the bird was generally silent, it had its own form of soundless communication, staring deeply into the eyes of its observers. The husband saw his wife's quiet intensity mirrored in the animal, to which she became increasingly attached. It had spectacularly colored plumage and stood regally on its perch. She kept it in a cage in the kitchen and would speak to it every time she passed. It would stare, occasionally cocking its head.

One day, the woman came home in tears. Her supervisor had unjustly blamed her for the loss of a major client. Feeling falsely accused, she left the office before lunch in shambles.

"I need to get out of here," she muttered agitatedly to the bird. "I want to change jobs, but have no other skills, I want to meet new people but I'm trapped by my relationship, I want to learn new things, but I'm afraid of starting from scratch, I want to grow a garden but I'm limited by this small space, and most of all, I just want to scream, but I know there's no one who will listen."

The bird cocked its head, and looked up at her. "That's quite a cage you've built for yourself," it said.

She looked at the small animal, eyes wide. "From the looks of it, you're the one in a cage," she retorted.

The bird paused, its black eyes fixed on her piercingly. "You've put me in one cage, but you've put yourself in four. Free me from mine, and maybe I'll free you from yours," it croaked.

Hesitantly, she lifted the latch on the door and the bird bolted through the kitchen and out the open window. As it fully spread its wings for the first time since being brought to their home, she saw that it had feathers, previously hidden from sight, that were the most beautiful mix of turquoise and gold. Those colors stayed in the back of her mind for sometime after the bird flew off into the distance.

Exhausted from crying, she went to bed early that night. The woman woke the next morning with the image of the bird floating off into the distance on her mind. It brought her back to memories of running around the living room as a child with the world at her feet, a feeling she had almost forgotten. Her husband groggily walked into the bedroom, returning from the kitchen with two mugs of coffee.

"I'm quitting my job today," she exclaimed, grinning. "I'm quitting my job, we're moving out of this apartment, and we're hitting the road." She was saying the first things that came to her mind, but for some reason, the idea seemed infinitely easier than spending even one more day in the office.

Her husband squinted at her, only half listening. "What happened to the bird?" he asked.

The Significance of Freedom

Freedom, in its most basic form, is our ability to choose. However, because choices reflect our individual values, freedom is also the capacity to act on our beliefs. It allows us to live meaningfully and intentionally. When we choose to spend time, effort, or resources on something, we are expressing a piece of ourselves. We're demonstrating the value and meaning that it has to us.

We show how meaningful our family is by choosing to spend our time with them. We show how precious our belongings are by choosing to keep them safe. We show how valuable our health is by choosing to exercise and eat well. The freedom to choose shapes our behavior, our environment, and our very identity. Without it, we wouldn't be able to express ourselves and our lives would feel out of our control.

Yet we rarely notice how our freedoms subtly change and shift. How certain activities put our freedoms in jeopardy or how creating freedom in one area can restrict it in another. When we rent a small city apartment, we increase our free time that may otherwise have been spent commuting, but limit the free space within which we can play or work at home. When we pursue financial freedom by remaining in a long-term, salaried job we reduce our freedom to explore new fields and discover hidden potential within ourselves. While none of these decisions are wrong, we should be aware of their effects so that we are able to make choices that reflect our ever-developing beliefs and values.

To consider the implications of freedom on our everyday lives, it's important to holistically understand what freedom is and what types of freedom exist. With this knowledge, we can decide for ourselves how we wish to cultivate it and when it can be sacrificed to further our other endeavors.

Physical Freedom

Perhaps the most obvious type of freedom relates to the *physical space* we have to move. How cramped are our living quarters? How restricted are our outdoor areas? Do we have room to do the things we love? Limitations to our physical freedom could come from cramped apartments, small office cubicles, or treadmills stuffed into corners of second-story one-room exercise facilities. So what are the implications of limited physical space?

Firstly, it restricts our ability to explore and discover new things about ourselves and our environments. When we live in a small apartment, we may feel that learning an instrument would be too bothersome to our neighbors, or that we can't stretch out enough to take up a yoga practice. This can cause us to get stuck in repetitive patterns of behavior, continuously doing what we know is possible, without any inspiration to explore. Internalizing these limited patterns of behavior may also create mental limitations that prevent us from moving even when space becomes available.

Imagine a vast physical space as a blank canvas on which we can paint anything we like. Having such a canvas both allows us to increase our artistic abilities, and brings us joy. Without a canvas, we may still be able to become artists. We could temporarily borrow materials from others or sketch our ideas in tiny notebooks, but this would be far more difficult. Physical space is a tool that enables us to think, grow, learn, explore, and enjoy. Restricting our ability to move freely takes that critical tool out of our box.

Secondly, anyone who has been into a pet store or animal shelter knows that animals don't fare well psychologically when confined. Dog trainer Caesar Milan notes in his book *Caesar's Way* that the dogs he encounters in the U.S. are riddled with psychological problems he never saw growing up on his family's farm in Mexico. He attributes this to the fact that cramped environments limit wholesome mental stimulation and ignore the natural evolutionary need to explore and coexist with nature. Cooped up animals become irrational and aggressive. Humans are no different, as we can observe in the people walking around crowded areas like lower Manhattan.

There grows within these individuals a deep longing for something outside their everyday lives and an ever-increasing frustration that change is unattainable. This frustration can quickly be turned outward as aggression and distrust, or taken inward as depression and anxiety. One of humanity's greatest delusions may be that we're different from animals. In reality, we're equally ill-equipped to tolerate physical restriction. Our only difference is how skilled we have become at rationalizing it.

A third challenge brought about by limited physical space manifests in how we interact with others. As we experience physical freedom decreasing, we put up mental barriers to compensate for the lost sense of privacy. When living in the Pennsylvania countryside, I knew each of my neighbors, despite some of their homes being a half-hour walk away. When living in a six-story walk-up in Manhattan, I didn't even know the name of the tenant across the hall. Ironically, being forced closer together can have the effect of pushing us further apart. Perhaps, this is because we tend to retreat inward for breathing room when there's none around us. When not done mindfully, this can lead to anti-social behavior, depression, loneliness, and anxiety, the epidemics of our modern day.

Struggling for personal space in cramped quarters can also lead us to lash out at those around us. We may yell at a neighbor whose music is too loud rather than approaching them caringly. We may create an irrational fear of strangers in our children rather than teaching them appropriate caution. These are all reactions to feeling trapped. They're defense mechanisms, compensating for situations that we often don't even realize we are in. Anyone who's lived with roommates can attest to the occasional defensive reaction that occurs when someone feels that their space was invaded. This shows that even those we know and love can become the targets of our harsh words and emotion.

When we have space, we have the physical freedom to be ourselves and pursue our desires. This enables us to interact with others from a place of personal security. We are no longer required to expend our mental energy fighting for elbow room. Instead we can use that energy to connect socially and explore. In this way, even a small amount of extra physical freedom can change our lives.

Operational Freedom

A second form of freedom involves our ability to choose what we *do* and how we *operate* in our lives. This operational freedom may be limited by our circumstances, the number of activities immediately available to us, or the perceived difficulty of new activities. For example, we may feel unable to pursue horseback riding because there are no ranches in our vicinity (limited availability), or because we believe we're not athletic enough (limited capacity), or because it's too expensive (limited resources). In the earlier parable, the accountant's perceived inability to change careers despite her unhappiness is a prime example of limited operational freedom.

Limits to operational freedom can exist on multiple levels. On a micro-level, they may manifest in our inability to do specific immediate activities. We may not be free to ride a bike on certain paths or talk in a performance space.

On a macro-level, operational freedom has a much greater significance, involving our perceived capacity to live according to our values. Feeling free to pursue a career in music may be a macro-level operational freedom limited by social pressures from family, or a lack of access to practice and recording space. Macro-level operational freedoms allow us to do what we love, change our paths, and self-determine our behaviors. Macro-operational freedom requires introspection to cultivate and offers the potential for impactful change when acted upon.

One of the most common perceived limitations to operational freedom comes as we advance down a specific path in life (such as a career or skilled hobby). As we gain education and experience, we increasingly commit to this chosen area of expertise and therefore feel less capable of deviating from that path. We may feel that it would take too long to build up new skills, that all the time we've spent would be wasted, or that we're simply unqualified for new experiences. Anxieties like these can be traps, preventing us from leaving unhealthy environments and living to our full potential.

Anxiety and fear naturally accompany feelings of limited opportunity. We may even fall into depression, believing that the future no longer holds anything new.

However, the most dangerous by-product of diminishing operational freedom is resentment. We may begin to resent ourselves for feeling unable to change our situation. We may begin to resent society for forcing us down our current path. We may begin to resent family, mentors, and friends who have lovingly provided us counsel, for contributing to our dissatisfaction. Lastly, we may begin to resent our past, present, and future; what's happened to us, what's happening to us, and where we feel we will inevitably end up.

This can be particularly dangerous as it leads to us believing the narrative of our life is beyond our control. These psychological effects are subtle and difficult to notice, until they've built up to a tipping point. It then becomes incredibly difficult to take responsibility for creating change. Cultivating self-awareness is essential to identifying changing operational freedom. With realization and recognition, mental threats to well-being can be addressed before they become dire. Trusted friends and family, or other role-models can serve as gentle sounding boards during this type of self-reflection.

Luckily, *feeling* trapped is not the same as *being* trapped. It's rather a by-product of how we choose to view our lives and whether or not we're able to see our assets as well as our deficits. While certain opportunities may be difficult to pursue, they are rarely completely out of reach and can often be brought closer if we are able to creatively use our skills to get started.

I was once given some advice by a friend as he reflected back on his twenty-five plus year career in the financial services industry. He told me, "When you're young, you see doors of opportunity opening all around you; as you get older, you shift towards seeing them all begin to close." It was an interesting sentiment with seemingly inherent logic and sense to it. Yet, somehow it felt too difficult to accept.

His words brought me back to something my father

had told me about aging, years earlier. He said that as he got older he had to make a concerted effort to remain mentally young. Growing up in India and working his entire life in the academic fields of crisis management and environmental sustainability, he'd seen a lot of bleak and difficult problems and places. This taught him that you can't let your past be the sole determinant of your present. If you do, you carry the weight of the world on your shoulders. You fail to see with fresh eyes.

This led me to reexamine my friend's reflection. From one perspective, his statement made sense. His operational freedom felt limited by the time he had committed to his previous work, and by the standards of his younger self, many doors had closed. However, in that moment, he wasn't accounting for the fact that as certain doors from his past closed, others opened. He was counting his "open doors" by looking down a hallway that he built as a 25-year-old, not observing the other hallways, buildings, and entire cities that had continuously developed around him through the years.

The closing of doors is a product of our mentality. While this may be linked to age, it is not determined by it. Since our age increases automatically and constantly, our mentalities must remain agile to keep pace. We must continue to see the world in new ways so that we can avoid becoming jaded. Such tiresome and negative mentalities are a needless punishment we inflict upon ourselves for aging. However, with a mindset centered around growth and rooted in the present, new doors will always continue to open. The world's infinite opportunity will always remain at hand.

To better understand, it may be helpful to think about these metaphorical buildings being constructed outside our hallway of closing doors. This echoes back to our short-term "doing" and long-term "being" goals. When we're young, our view of opportunity is focused on things we can *do*. It exists in terms of jobs we may hold, schools we may attend, and places we may go. Those types of opportunities comprise the doors we see as open to us. As we get older, priorities may shift, allowing us to focus more on things we can *be*.

We begin to see new doors and desires such as being a loving family member, a responsible citizen, or an expressive artist. If our first hallway of doors was in the building of "doing," the solidified sense of identity that comes with age builds us a second hallway in the building of "being." This is one way in which our opportunities may expand.

Secondly, as we gain experience we begin to understand the complexity of the world. This presents us with opportunities we may not have known to exist when we were young. We discover technical specialties that address niche fields and needs that were not presented in college career fairs. These could be considered "hidden doors" of opportunity.

Thirdly, we develop discipline and patience – two important qualities for success in any field. When we are young, we rarely have enough discipline or patience to be truly impactful. Approaching the doors to being great leaders, professionals, and change-makers requires these qualities, meaning despite the seeming freedom of youth, many doors to success are not unlocked until later in life.

We tend think of youth as a time of boundless *opportunity*, when in reality, its strongest advantage is *time*. But what can we do with that time when we don't have the knowledge to see our options, the priorities to choose them, the discipline to pursue them, the resources to invest in ourselves, or the reputation and respect to mobilize others? Youth is wonderful; however old age is also wonderful. Doors will always be closing and opening. In fact, we need some doors to close to allow others to open. It's only when we stare too closely at the closed doors, that we fail to see the new ones.

Qualifications

Another reason we feel limited in our operational freedom as we get older is our tendency to undervalue our qualifications. In the U.S., we tend to view qualifications in terms of *past accomplishment*, rather than *current capacity*. We look at university degrees based on where and when they were earned and view work experience in terms of what titles we've held and the number of years we've worked. While these milestones all represent experiences, they fall short of describing present capacities. Furthermore, they trap us in positions thematically similar to where we've already been.

By shifting our focus towards our current capacity, we remove this limitation. This doesn't mean we forget our past, but rather shift from thinking about our accomplishments, to thinking about what we can do, in the present, as a result of our accomplishments. This way we can shine a light on the learning that resulted from experiences rather than the participation trophies we've received. We may focus on our ability to conduct research rather than our earned degree or our skills as a facilitator rather than the number of conferences at which we've moderated discussions.

This isn't meant to be a new way to write a resume or pitch ourselves to others. This information is already commonly included on resumes and combined with facts on where we have worked and studied. Instead, this is a new way for us, as individuals, to think about the options that are available to us. It is a mentality that increases our sense of operational freedom. Even when we're well aware of our capabilities, we often still fail to see the diversity of options that they create for us. This small shift in thinking can move us from believing that our four-year degree in English literature means we are going to be a teacher, to seeing choices in other areas such as marketing, proposal writing for non-profits, adventure blogging, or advocacy work.

The fact that we all have widely applicable skills is not revolutionary, however it shows that when we feel trapped we can shift the weight off our past direction and open opportunities based on our present needs and desires. We can create space for ourselves to think creatively about the future.

Interestingly, making this shift can have a fundamental impact on how we learn by encouraging us to engage mindfully in experiences so that we come away with non-material value (in the form of skills and education). It changes an activity from being a means to an end (attending class for a certificate) to an end in and of itself (attending class to learn). It's the difference between reading a book to say that you've finished it and reading to further your understanding of a topic. When we live presently, we understand that the past only matters to the extent that we decide to carry it with us.

Thinking in this way allows us to maintain a growth mindset that encourages life-long learning. When we conceptualize our identities based on past accomplishment, we subject ourselves to the most conventional path of education. We graduate high school, maybe college, maybe graduate school, we take an entry-level job, hit our five-year or maybe ten-year anniversary, and then our period of learning ends. We've checked the boxes on our learning agenda and given ourselves the resume lines that say "I have learned".

However, learning doesn't need to, and shouldn't, end there. When we see ourselves as we are in the present, rather than as a collection of our past experiences, we will never reach a point where "learning" has been accomplished. We're constantly able to reassess our abilities and develop them, or cultivate new ones. We aren't preoccupied with looking at our trophies, but rather focused on using fresh eyes to look at ourselves. This allows us to maneuver in different directions and remain operationally free. With such a mindset, we begin to see aspects of our education that have connections across disciplines, uncovering unforeseen paths to continuing our education and redefining the metrics with which we measure our progress.

As an exercise, consider what you'd be able to do if you were left possession-less in a foreign land. What skills, knowledge, and experience would you carry internally, separate from qualifying institutions or reputation? What could you offer to others? What would allow you to succeed? What would give your new life meaning and purpose? These answers are our true qualifications, beyond any resume or certificate. Recognizing these practical qualifications can free us operationally, allowing us to pursue the lives we desire.

We should always appreciate and celebrate our accomplishments. We deserve to feel satisfied by, and commemorate, our hard work. Failing to do so often works against our sense of operational freedom, feeding our underlying insecurities. However, we must not let these memories or tokens of past accomplishment eclipse our present ability or desire to improve.

In nature, an animal's worth is measured by its ability to provide and protect, rather than its past accomplishments. Foxes don't collect the tails of the rodents they've caught, gulls don't color their feathers for each migratory path they learn, and ants don't wear badges to mark battles they've won or hills they've built. Using tokens of past accomplishment to judge self-worth is a uniquely human practice that leads to anxiety, self-criticism and the mischaracterization of capability. If like foxes, gulls, and ants, we can move away from conceptualizing ourselves as a collection of trophies and towards focusing on our present abilities, we may realize that we're capable of a lot more than we thought possible.

FREEDOM

Fear and Failure

An understandable barrier to expanding operational freedom and personal growth is our inherent and compulsive fear of failure. As children we become accustomed to failure. We're desensitized to looking silly or coming in last because so much of what we do is completely new to us. This gives us the ability to fearlessly approach diverse experiences, and is perhaps why we feel that we have so much opportunity as children.

As we age, this ability decreases – out of choice, rather than necessity. We determine what we're good at, then selectively pursue those activities. We forget what it feels like to fail, until we reach the point where even the idea of failure feels deeply disturbing. We then begin to shy away from new experiences to avoid trauma. By adulthood, we too often see fear and embarrassment as out of the question, removing all options outside our established comfort zone. With this mindset, it's no wonder we feel as though opportunities have become limited to us. We've fallen into our own trap, and it will continue to close around us until *we* decide to reopen it.

Even child psychologists have moved away from telling children they are the best, in lieu of commending their hard work and persistence. Adults must also encourage themselves in this way. Rather than focusing on the end goal of success, we can strive to realize a path of growth and learning, despite the inevitable existence of intermittent failure. In a sense, failure is the action that we must do, repetitively and persistently, to achieve success. When we become unable to fail, we become limited to the things we've already had the courage to fail at earlier in our lives.

Emotional Freedom

If physical and operational freedom determine what we can do, emotional freedom determines how we do it. That is to say, how free we are to *express* ourselves in our daily lives. Emotional freedom dictates the extent to which we're able to act while accurately representing and expressing our individual identities. In other words, *how true to ourselves we're able to be.*

While physical and operational freedoms are usually limited by either our physical surroundings or individual mentalities, emotional freedom faces an additional limitation imposed by our social environments. Since a large part of identity is formed through social affiliation, our peer groups naturally have a strong influence over our behavior. This influence can be either positive or negative, depending on the extent to which we agree with our peers' beliefs and values. For example, combing our hair and wearing a suit could be a positive behavioral change prompted by others in the workplace, whereas treating other employees disrespectfully to appear powerful may be a negative behavioral change.

We often make these behavioral adjustments subconsciously without reflecting on why we're acting differently or what the impacts of our actions are. When such changes are incongruent with our personal beliefs, they restrict our ability to behave outwardly as we feel internally. This limits our emotional freedom. Slowly, our capacity for emotional self-expression is smothered.

As an undergraduate student, I can clearly remember feeling limited in my emotional freedom. I lived in a large fraternity house (physical freedom) with several career options (operational freedom), however the pressure to conform to the norms of my peer group almost completely eclipsed my ability to behave according to my own beliefs and identity. This limited freedom of expression led to many destructive behaviors.

In our house, there were things that could be said and done, and things that could not. The rules were set by the collective and those who transgressed were ridiculed until they either left or conformed. At first, it all seemed acceptable. It almost felt like an interesting cross-cultural learning experience. Mindlessly, I followed suit, slowly and unconsciously adjusting my own behavior.

Four years later, I found myself drunkenly sitting at my graduation ceremony, sobbing over a girl while intermittently heckling the speaker. While I'd like to say that I wasn't being myself, by that point I'd behaved like other people for so long that I didn't even know who I was. I had warped my identity into an amalgam of collective immorality, self-loathing, and over-rationalization, desperately trying to reconcile my behavior with my supposed beliefs. My ability to express myself emotionally had been completely suppressed. Unfortunately, this is an all too common example of limited emotional freedom and its effects. Experiences like these lead us to feel alone, because no one really knows us; conflicted, because we are not acting on our beliefs; and trapped, because we don't feel capable of breaking the behavioral patterns we've developed.

Surprisingly, while living in Senegal, and later in Liberia, I experienced similar sacrifices in emotional freedom. Although the social pressures in these environments were far less destructive, the effects were equally as intense. I lived in remote, deeply religious communities where I took on local names, spoke in local dialects, and severely censored myself to remain influential and respected. I did this out of fear that expressing my individual identity would highlight the fact that I shared few personal similarities with other community members. I worried that being too unrelatable would make me less effective in my work.

I believed I was sacrificing my emotional freedom to

maintain my operational freedom, feeling that the two were at odds with one another. Looking back, I'm still not sure if that feeling was justified. What I am sure of, is that very few of my friends and community members knew the real me, which had a profound impact on my mental well-being.

Over the course of our lives, we'll be repeatedly required to make the choice between being ourselves and who others want us to be. In reality, both options present benefits and difficulties, and each individual must choose the path they deem best. However, it's important to take into consideration the long and short-term implications of this choice each time we make it so that we understand where our behaviors will lead us. Understanding both the causes and effects of our actions in this way allows us to shift from being victims of external influences to the masters of our own destinies. As such, we can be confident in what we believe and assure that we remain authentic.

Comfortably Uncomfortable

A key component of maintaining emotional freedom is the level of social comfort we feel in our environment. This is often dependent upon the extent to which we feel accepted by others and able to express ourselves without the fear of negative consequences. Uncomfortable situations discourage us from showing our authentic selves out of fear that we won't be accepted.

Unfortunately, environments in which we feel comfortable and able to easily express ourselves, are rarely those that push us to grow, learn, and develop. They fail to give us challenges that encourage us to evaluate our behaviors and beliefs, or provide the diversity needed to introduce new world-views and opinions. Reconciling the need to venture out of our comfort zones (where we can grow) with the need to feel comfortable enough to express ourselves (where we have emotional freedom) is therefore quite challenging.

Fortunately, these needs can be balanced. When we venture into the unknown, feel discomfort, and experience restricted emotional freedom, we can adapt by making the unfamiliar familiar and the uncomfortable comfortable. As we leave our comfort zone, it begins to adjust and expand. By the time we feel that a new experience has benefited us, we've assimilated it into our understanding of the world. It is no longer foreign. We've grown.

Emotional freedom comes naturally when we're around those who accept us. However, true self-confidence is built when we learn to genuinely express ourselves around people who aren't naturally accepting. This requires us to have an *internal sense of comfort* that we carry around with us wherever we go, rather than *relying on our environment* to make us feel at ease. In my undergraduate experience, this may have meant slowly showing my peers who I was rather than slowly becoming who they were. In my experiences in Africa, this may have meant slowly revealing my culture until it was accepted rather than wholeheartedly conforming to my community's norms.

This internal comfort is challenged often in our lives to various degrees and in diverse circumstances. Responding to these challenges requires a nuanced understanding of ourselves and our situations. Pursuing such understanding is a journey that will continue for as long as we continue to learn and grow.

So how can we make uncomfortable environments into places where we're able to express ourselves and maintain emotional freedom? To start, we can find ways to strategically and intentionally inject our unique identities in our social groups. We need to shift our self-conception from "the influenced" to "the influencers." Group culture is fluid, yet we often see it as fixed. We don't realize that it's an amalgam of each participating individual's personality, and that it is our choice to follow or redefine that group dynamic. This shows us that emotional freedom isn't something that's given by our environment, but rather created by our individual behavior.

To influence our social groups, we first need to overcome our fears of being inappropriate or unaccepted. A few years ago, I was talking to some fellow boxers in our gym locker room. Mid-way through the conversation, a romance novel fell out of one man's open locker. The group jeered and he turned bright red. While I'd seen him reading the novel earlier that week, he denied that it was even his. It was clear that the hyper-masculine environment restricted the emotional freedom he needed to share his hobby.

What would have happened if he had admitted he liked romance novels? Perhaps nothing. Perhaps he would have been ridiculed further. Perhaps he would have discovered that others shared his interest but were also scared to admit it. Although there was a strong preexisting gym culture, it was perpetuated and defined by group members including him and me. We had the power to redefine it according to our own beliefs.

While it seemed as though his environment limited the extent to which he could express himself, the greater limitation was his discomfort. His embarrassment had validated the group's impression that romance novels were silly, whereas his confidence, combined with a little support, could have changed that impression. Owning and openly endorsing his interest would have been an impactful means of creating emotional freedom. Exposing our true thoughts and beliefs is difficult, however once we put them out there, it gets easier each time. The more we share, the freer we become. The freer we are, the more we are able to pave the way for others to also feel comfortable expressing themselves.

FREEDOM

Mental Freedom

Our final type of freedom describes the existence of mental space. It involves our ability to sometimes feel aimless and objectiveless, in contrast to our usual purpose-driven lives. While other freedoms enable us to act (to move, pursue, and express), mental freedom enables us to wander. It's the absence of distraction that lets us stop, rest, and openly reflect.

When our minds are overstimulated, we often cease to look and think deeply about where we want to go or what we want to do. Decisions are made quickly using the small amount of free mental processing power we have available. Limited mental freedom doesn't necessarily reduce operational freedom, because it doesn't make us feel as though we *can't* maneuver. Instead, it prompts us to act without reflection; to move forward mindlessly.

When we hear of someone having a mid-life crisis, it's sometimes the result of lacking mental freedom. In such cases, individuals have pushed their lives forward tirelessly with no time to fully pause and think, no period without an overarching goal or stopping point. This causes extreme and sudden life changes when they begin to question why they're on their path. Insufficient space to explore and discover builds up tension. To release this tension, we overcompensate with bizarre and unforeseen changes. Perhaps we realize that we've spent too long in our offices, so we buy a motorcycle and hit the open road. Perhaps we feel we've been too financially conservative so we move our savings into crypto currency. These "crises" allow us to regain our feelings of control and intentionality. By cultivating mental freedom, we can release tensions before they build to a bursting point. We can learn to intermittently step away and gain perspective, allowing ourselves to gauge our feelings and evaluate the paths we've chosen.

Mental freedom can also impact our creativity. As perpetual consumers, we tend to adopt preferences, practices, and interests related to the content we consume. These fill our mental space, until there is no room for individual reflection or creativity. We see that the reputable anchor on the news wears a striped tie, so we wear striped ties; we hear our colleagues talking about a new bestselling book, so we begin to spread the word; we observe how our friends use social media, so we follow suit. It's normal. However, when unchecked, it can stop us from thinking about the reasoning behind our behavior. We cease to reflect on what we think looks best, what opinions we believe to be right, or how we wish to connect and communicate. Instead, our distractions automatically dictate these answers. Mental freedom, therefore, sometimes means turning off and doing nothing. It means giving ourselves the quiet and calm needed to clearly see and focus on our own individual preferences, interests, and beliefs - uninfluenced.

The cultural isolation and lack of internet connectivity I experienced in rural West Africa gave me my first real taste of mental freedom. I'd been writing and making music all my life, yet failing to find an original voice. It wasn't until I was forced to separate from the connected world that I understood why. Without distraction, my art began to reflect my thoughts and immediate surroundings rather than regurgitating pop culture and social media. This brought new meaning and ingenuity. When I was able to stop looking to the world for cues, I finally got the feeling that I, as an individual, had something to say. This voice can only come from a quiet mind with space to explore.

The clarity created by mental freedom can be compared to the difference between intoxication and sobriety. When intoxicated, it's easy to create in quantity, make quick decisions, and feel confident in what we're doing. We can talk endlessly and argue relentlessly. However, our conversations lack quality, our decisions lack foresight, and our confidence is fleeting. When we lack the mental space to reflect and sit quietly with ourselves, we begin to simply repeat what we see and spread what others tell us. Our creations lack quality because they lack originality, our decisions lack foresight because we're focused on immediacy, and our confidence is fleeting because it's given to us rather than created by us. Meaningful, skillfully crafted creations, whether they be life decisions, art, or conversation are seldom created under the condition of limited mental freedom.

When we are undistracted, with time to spare and space to reflect, we give our lives, our art, and our choices the attention they need to be meaningful, effective, and reflective of our true selves. Sometimes we need a blank canvas to know what painting we want to create. In this way, we understand that it isn't until you stop doing everything that you become able to start doing anything.

It Takes Room to Tango

While I was living in Liberia, I adopted a puppy from a local farmer. The tiny animal had been living in squalor, infested with worms, and on the verge of starvation. I took him in, named him Tango, and slowly nursed him back to health.

After a few months Tango was following me everywhere and adamantly refused to leave my side. At work, he would sit at my feet; at home, he would sit under my desk; and at night, he would sleep by my bed. Tango didn't seem to stay so close due to fear of the outside world but rather out of affection for his pack. He was friendly with the neighbors (a rare quality in Liberian dogs who are often fearful and weary) and quickly became well known in the community. Ultimately, Tango was like an American dog for the first six months of his life. He was kept in a safe environment, with ample food and toys, regular walks, and predominately human attention.

However, the level of safety that allowed Tango to recover and thrive in terms of his physical health also came with limitations. While he was sometimes allowed to roam the neighborhood, he was normally confined to my house or office, and on walks, even when off the leash, he had to stay nearby. While he could play with other dogs, I would always supervise so he would avoid those that looked sickly or mangy.

While these precautions were for his own benefit, I could tell that Tango wondered why these limitations weren't imposed on the other animals around him. Other dogs were free. Granted they had to fight for their territory, scrounge for their food, sleep outside, and avoid being kidnapped and eaten…but what Tango saw was their freedom.

When Tango was about six months old I took a two-week vacation. It was the longest time we'd been apart since I took him home. I let him stay with my close Liberian friend who owned a small farm inside a densely populated rural neighborhood. Her family was caring, intelligent, and loved Tango, yet I was worried about the rural Liberian cultural practices concerning pet care. In our neighborhood, dogs would usually sleep outside, roam the surrounding area, and eat by scrounging for leftovers or trash.

Nevertheless, I gave my friend a few important tips on feeding and a big bag of dog food, insisted that Tango sleep inside, and then left for my vacation. When I returned two weeks later, Tango was looking safe and happy. He greeted me excitedly while also showing great affection for his temporary caretakers. However, upon a closer inspection I saw that he had small burn marks under his legs, swollen red bumps on two of his feet, a chipped tooth, and numerous fleas (granted he always had a few under my care, since anti-flea medications were scarce).

Of course, none of this was intentional, he had simply been sniffing around coal cooking fires, chewing on everything he could find, and rolling around in the dirt all day. In fact, he'd loved it. Despite being happy to see me, he returned on his own to his "other family" the first night after I came back.

It felt to me as if part of Tango had returned to the wild. At heart, he was still a domestic animal, but his situation had allowed him to see the benefits and shortcomings of two very different lifestyles. Judging by his behavior over the next few weeks, it appeared he didn't feel that sacrifices for comfort and safety were worth his freedom; a choice which his animal brain made automatically. Limits to his physical freedom imposed at my house caused almost neurotic behavior when compared to the time he spent outside. Limits to his operational freedom led him to stare longingly at the animals roaming around the trash dumps visible from my front porch. I saw that my life, which would one day bring me back to the States and into a cramped apartment, couldn't provide Tango with the freedoms he needed to be happy. He now lives on my friend's farm, free to roam and surrounded by family, where he may live a shorter but more satisfying "dog life."

I tell Tango's story, because he made me realize how important freedom is and how easily animals will choose freedom, despite its risks, when given the opportunity. That's a choice we can learn from. We justify restricted freedoms, for the sake of safety, comfort, ease, or security, when in reality, these needs are not mutually exclusive. We need them all, freedom included.

Space and Mindfulness

With these types of freedom in mind, I'd like to revisit two ideas: *space* and *mindfulness*. Space exists in multiple dimensions. It can be internal, external, philosophical, physical, and metaphysical. It is, in the very broadest sense, the essence comprising wherever we are. When we're depressed, our emotions exist within a dark mental space, when we're confined, our body exists in a cramped physical space, when we're confused, our thoughts exist within a crowded intellectual space, and when we feel belonging, our spirit exists within a harmonious communal space.

Mindfulness, on the other hand, entails how we experience that space. It's our perception of reality – how we observe and interpret the space we're in. Together, space and mindfulness form the basic building blocks of freedom. They allow us to remove the layers of complexity clouding our perception, enabling us to navigate the world with clear minds and open hearts.

Space is integral to each of our freedoms. Physical freedom necessitates immediate physical space, operational freedom requires space to maneuver, emotional freedom requires a space in which we feel comfortable expressing ourselves, and mental freedom is defined by the calm brought through the existence of empty space.

The underlying condition of space allows us to have the maneuverability that we call freedom. Therefore, we can strive to create space when the idea of creating freedom feels too abstract or unattainable. By mindfully observing the effect that our attempts to create freedom have on our space, we can gauge their overall efficacy and impact.

Mindfulness is clarity and insight. Cultivating mindfulness entails becoming aware of the way we relate to and navigate space. This isn't only essential to cultivating freedom, but to all forms of self-improvement. We need an honest understanding of our perceptions, and an honest understanding of ourselves, to know where we can improve and how to get where we want to go. Mindfulness itself isn't freedom, but it allows us to see where our freedoms exist and where they are restricted. It allows us to see the world around us and our relationship to it. Through engaging mindfully when deciding where to live, how to occupy our time, who to be around, and who we want to become, we can prevent those decisions from limiting our freedoms and our overall happiness. This is especially important in a world of unparalleled influencers and advertisers. Mindfulness assures that we are the deciding factor in the choices we make.

Complexity

Freedoms are complex, nuanced, and closely interwoven. However, this doesn't mean that having one type of freedom automatically assures us others. We can feel trapped physically but emotionally free, or trapped operationally but mentally free.

An inmate who has undergone a spiritual awakening may feel a new freedom of self-expression (emotional freedom) despite confined quarters (restricted physical freedom); a sailor at sea may turn to deep introspection (mental freedom) when there are few other available activities (restricted operational freedom); a corporate executive in a large and beautiful home (physical freedom) may feel forced to continue on the same path all their life (restricted operational freedom); a young adult may choose a career (operational freedom) having never been taught self-awareness or self-expression (restricted emotional freedom).

Recognizing areas in which we feel trapped is an important learning experience. We often falsely think that "being trapped" is the opposite of "being free." This is an unfortunate misunderstanding. Being trapped is rather the key to understanding what it means to be free. One cannot exist without the other. We strive and advocate for freedom, only because we've felt trapped in the past. Those moments have allowed us to recognize aspects of our lives that we've needed to change and improve. Feeling trapped is an indicator. Like a canary in a coal mine, it alerts us when danger is near. As we gain certain freedoms, others may become limited, and feeling trapped will naturally accompany those limitations. Recognizing those feelings will allow us to reflect and readjust. They aren't cause to panic or quit, but rather a call to breath deeply and create change.

The existence of freedom along so many dimensions means we often need to view our lives from different perspectives. We need to understand that the word "freedom" is relative, and accept the possibility that complete freedom may be unattainable. It is complex, ambiguous, and ever-evolving. Endless terms and metrics will only ever provide us partial insight. So we must temper our understanding with instinct as we strive to remain free.

CONCLUSION

An Intricate Web

No concepts in this book exist independently of one another. Presence builds freedom and is the necessary mindset for adventure. Freedom creates space for adventure and eliminates barriers that may otherwise bring us into a waiting mindset.

Returning to the wild is not a step-by-step process, or checklist to complete, but rather an understanding of the intricate web of factors that can positively impact us. It is understanding that once one quality, whether it be presence, connection, adventure, or freedom, is touched, they're all touched. When one is reinforced, it opens the door to the others. It's a system that can only be approached and adopted in its totality, simply because it only exists as the sum of its component parts.

The Small Dirt Path

There was once a man who lived with his dog in a small seaside town. They walked each morning along the cliffs by the shore, watching the waves create bursts of foam akin to gently floating cumulus clouds as they crashed into the jagged rocks below. The man looked at the long fall down into the frothy waters and thought of his own death.

He regretted not living up to the high expectations his family had once had for him. He felt trapped by his own ineptitude, having retreated to the coast after failing to attend medical school as his brother had or find success in industry like his younger sister. It weighed on him, creating a tightness in his chest, which he feared to share, even with the dog looking sullenly up at him from below, eyes sunken and mouth resting in a lazy smile.

He'd taken this walk each day for years and now knew each patch of grass and stump along the way. He knew how far he could go before getting hungry and where he could rest without getting dirt on his clothing. And so, he marched on, mechanically grinding away the hour and twenty-three minutes before he would once again reach home.

He knew the dog well. It had accompanied him on his walk for as long as he'd lived in his house by the shore. Sometimes neighbors would also join, thinking he was a strange man, and reaching out in misplaced charitable attempts to provide company. He would end his walk early on such days, guiding them through some neighboring farmland on a shortcut home, then thanking them half-heartedly before hurrying inside.

The dogs ears perked up as it caught a mysterious scent in the air. It heard the grasses to its left whisper in the wind. The gale carried a delightfully unrecognizable scent, hinting at a surprise hidden about fifteen feet away. It relished both the smell and the accompanying enigma. It pondered chasing down the scent, ultimately deciding to return later. There were many mysterious smells along the path, each bringing new excitement and intrigue. It was the dog's solemn task to choose which to pursue and when. At times, it would follow a smell for what felt like miles, only to fall into a porcupine's angry quills or slip into a hidden foxhole. Nevertheless, it boldly sought out the next lead, pursuing those worthy with both vigor and determination.

The dog loved the man who walked beside it. And similarly, the porcupines that would mistakenly impale it with quills, the foxes that dug holes for their families, and the neighbors from nearby homes that occasionally took their time to join in meandering along the cliffside. This was, indeed, a particularly beautiful morning, the dog thought to itself, merrily trotting along.

Behind the two, the small dirt path stretched

backwards into the distance. After they passed, the grass still whispered in the wind, the waves still crashed onto the rocks, and the clouds continued to move idly overhead. Sounds of nature drifted through the air, bearing no meaning beyond what a man or dog might someday assign them as they walked by, caught up in worlds of their own creation.

FERAL

EPILOGUE

This book represents my truth, formed from my small glimpse at a very large world. It draws from the field of conflict resolution and my travels as a conflict resolution and international development practitioner. Having shared my perspective, I invite you to reach out and share your own impressions, experiences, and ideas. Like this, hopefully we may all come to interpret the sounds of nature as calls back to the wild, as we venture to become the dog rather than the man walking by its side.

KYLE COOPER SHRIVASTAVA

FERAL

Kyle Cooper Shrivastava is a peace builder on the Global Initiatives Team at **Partners**Global where he helps implement projects to improve the resiliency of global civil society. He is also a co-founder of R3SOLUTE, a Berlin-based non-profit that teaches conflict resolution and peer mediation skills to refugees. He received his M.S. in conflict resolution from Columbia University, and has served with the Peace Corps in both Senegal and Liberia. He currently lives with his girlfriend in Washington D.C.

ReturningtotheWild.com

www.ingramcontent.com/pod-product-compliance
Lightning Source LLC
Chambersburg PA
CBHW051637050426
42443CB00025B/402